FUNDAMENTALISM

Smyth & Helwys Publishing, Inc.
6316 Peake Road
Macon, Georgia 31210-3960
1-800-747-3016
©2004 by Smyth & Helwys Publishing
All rights reserved.
Printed in the United States of America.

The paper used in this publication meets the minimum requirements of
American National Standard for Information Sciences—
Permanence of Paper for Printed Library Materials.
ANSI Z39.48–1984. (alk. paper)

Library of Congress Cataloging-in-Publication Data

Humphreys, Fisher.
Fundamentalism
by Fisher Humphreys and Philip Wise.
p. cm.
Includes bibliographical references.
ISBN 1-57312-398-6 (pbk. : alk. paper)
1. Fundamentalism.
I. Wise, Philip.
II. Title.
BT82.2.H86 2004
270.8'2–dc22

2004003979

FUNDAMENTALISM

Fisher Humphreys

and

Philip Wise

SMYTH&HELWYS
PUBLISHING, INCORPORATED   MACON, GEORGIA

Dedication

*To the Cooperative Baptist Fellowship and
to President Jimmy Carter*

CONTENTS

Preface vii

Foreword ix

Introduction: Getting Our Bearings 1

Chapter 1: Generic Fundamentalism 9

Chapter 2: The Original Fundamentalism 17

Chapter 3: The Theology of Fundamentalism 35

Chapter 4: The Attitudes of Fundamentalism.....................57

Chapter 5: Fundamentalism and Southern Baptists 65

Chapter 6: Relating to Fundamentalists 81

Conclusion: A Better Way 91

Discussion Guide 101

PREFACE

As we wrote this book, we discussed it with numerous friends, and we are grateful to them for their ideas. Two of them went the extra mile of reading a draft of the manuscript, and we want to offer them a special word of thanks; they are Dr. Paul Basden and Dr. Samuel J. Mikolaski. In 2003 we led two breakout sessions at the General Assembly of the Cooperative Baptist Fellowship, and our discussions with participants in those workshops were helpful to us. The responsibility for what we have written is, of course, ours.

Scripture quotations are from the New Revised Standard Version, except where otherwise noted.

We dedicate this book to an organization and an individual who for us represent public examples of what it means to follow the way of Jesus Christ. Their lives display the richness of Christian life without Fundamentalism.

FOREWORD

Fisher Humphreys and Philip Wise have rendered a great service. Writing primarily for non-fundamentalist Christians in the United States, they have developed a much-needed resource for a considerably wider audience. Many people—journalists, political leaders, people of faith from other traditions, and people who don't identify with any religious tradition—will benefit greatly from the clear, accessible, and fair-minded approach in this short volume. Without rancor or polemics, Humphreys and Wise offer insight and understanding where presuppositions and passions frequently produce far more heat than light.

Fundamentalism is now a prominent part of the religious and political landscape. The term is used widely and loosely to characterize a range of people, groups, and movements all over the world. While there are common features among diverse, contemporary movements in many religious traditions, the casual use of this term can easily be misleading. Humphreys and Wise clarify the differences and relationships among evangelical and fundamentalist Christians even as they provide an interpretative framework for global phenomena. In the process, they include helpful resources for more in-depth study.

The importance of clear thinking about fundamentalism at this pivotal time in world history cannot be overstated. The stakes are high. The dangers posed by religiously motivated extremists are evident on the front pages of daily newspapers. Fundamentalism demands a rigid certainty that can easily lead to a dangerous kind of zealotry. Absolute truth claims too often embolden religious extremists to see themselves as instruments of God's will amid perceived injustice. When the defenders of God's truth include justification for violent and destructive behavior, you have a recipe for disaster. In the aftermath of September 11, 2001, the dangers associated with religious zealotry are crystal clear. We now know with certainty that there are many weapons of mass destruction in our world—chemical, biological, and nuclear weapons as well as many "weapons" (like commercial airliners turned into bombs) we hadn't considered previously. We now know with certainty that it doesn't take many people to wreak havoc on a global scale.

The invitation to understand fundamentalism and fundamentalists more accurately is also an invitation to self-critical awareness. Fundamentalists say, for example, that they interpret the Bible literally. Despite claims to the contrary, Christian fundamentalists read and interpret sacred texts selectively. How do you take the Song of Songs literally? This erotic poem celebrating love between and man and a woman does not even mention God. It is generally understood as a metaphor for God's love for Israel or the Church. A metaphor is not a literal interpretation, however. The legal codes of Leviticus are not taken literally by Christians or Jews today. Many biblical passages—from prophetic books to parables of Jesus—are interpreted in different ways, depending on the lens or frame of reference employed by the adherent. In fact, people in all religious traditions appropriate sacred texts selectively, though not always self-consciously. Humphreys and Wise call their readers to think clearly and self-critically about these and other important issues where different understandings can lead to significantly different outcomes.

The authors remind us that no one has everything locked down. As human beings, we do not possess the mind of God. In the words of the apostle Paul to the Corinthians, "We see through a glass dimly, not yet face to face." At best, we have a "treasure in earthen vessels." We are all on a journey, a lifelong process of growing, learning, unlearning, and changing. Through the lens of this study, Humphreys and Wise underscore that one can be a person of faith with depth, commitment, and sincerity while at the same time recognizing that there is much more to learn.

This book will not only benefit many individuals; it is also ideal for serious adult study programs in churches. It is my hope that it will be used widely in this way. Not only will it facilitate much-needed conversation about Fundamentalism, but congregational study of this book will encourage thoughtful, self-critical reflection and constructive action on a range of issues that challenge all of us in an increasingly interdependent and interconnected world community.

The book concludes with a particular concern for progressive Baptists. Humphreys and Wise gently explain how "the Fundamentalist impulse and movement have tended to miss the fundamentals of the Christian faith and to work against the unity and harmony of the church." They encourage a broader, more ecumenical approach, one that embraces diversity among Christians while affirming central teachings. In a word, they model an approach to faith that humbly seeks to love God and love one's neighbor.

Charles Kimball, Author of *When Religion Becomes Evil*

GETTING OUR BEARINGS

In fall 2001, Beeson Divinity School in Birmingham, Alabama, sponsored a conference called "Pilgrims on the Sawdust Trail." The speakers included Roman Catholics, mainline Protestants, evangelical Protestants, Pentecostals, and Anglicans. There also was one Fundamentalist speaker, Dr. Kevin T. Bauder of Central Baptist Seminary in Plymouth, Minnesota.[1] Dr. Bauder gave a persuasive lecture, and he responded ably to questions from other speakers and from the people attending the conference. He made a strong case not only for believing and preaching the fundamentals of the Christian faith, but for defending them in the way Fundamentalism has done throughout its history.

After the conference, one of us (Fisher) initiated discussions with his students who had attended the conference. The students asked questions such as these: "What makes Fundamentalism different from other expressions of Christianity?" "Why would any Christian not want to be a Fundamentalist?" "Why do other Christians criticize Fundamentalists so much?" These are good questions, and in this book we will do our best to answer them.

Our Readers

We wrote this book with a particular audience in mind, and we want to describe that audience as clearly as possible.

To begin with, we have not written our book for Fundamentalists. Knowledgeable and committed Fundamentalists probably wouldn't benefit from reading this book. We have not tried to help Fundamentalists gain a better understanding of their Christian faith, and we have not attempted to argue Fundamentalists out of their Fundamentalism. There is a vast literature of polemics between Fundamentalists and those who disagree with them; we have no desire to contribute to that literature.

On the other hand, we believe that those who read a book about Fundamentalism need to know that this expression of Christian faith evokes powerful, negative reactions; it would be a disservice to our readers if we did not provide them with some sense of the way in which many observers feel about Fundamentalism, so we offer the following as an example:

> One of the most startling developments of the late twentieth century has been the emergence within every major religious tradition of a militant piety popularly known as "fundamentalism." Its manifestations are sometimes shocking. Fundamentalists have gunned down worshipers in a mosque, have killed doctors and nurses who work in abortion clinics, have shot their presidents, and have even toppled a powerful government. It is only a small minority of fundamentalists who commit such acts of terror, but even the most peaceful and law-abiding are perplexing, because they seem so adamantly opposed to many of the most positive values of modern society. Fundamentalists have no time for democracy, pluralism, religious toleration, peacekeeping, free speech, or the separation of church and state.[2]

We have quoted this passage, despite reservations about parts of it, because we believe the task of understanding and relating to Fundamentalism includes recognizing that it evokes passionate responses such as this from thoughtful and informed people.

We have not written our book for people who are contemptuous of Fundamentalism and would like to read a savage attack on Fundamentalism. We do not feel contempt for Fundamentalism. In fact, we think it is spiritually unhealthy for Christians to be contemptuous of the religious beliefs and practices of others, and we intend to encourage our readers to understand Fundamentalism sympathetically and to respect what is good in it.

We think it is regrettable that many people in America today feel contempt for Fundamentalism. Some of them have never encountered Fundamentalism firsthand but have read and heard things about it that make them fearful or distrustful of it. *The Poisonwood Bible* by Barbara Kingsolver[3] and *The Handmaid's Tale* by Margaret Atwood[4] are novels that portray some of the things people find frightening about Fundamentalism.

Some of those who feel contempt for Fundamentalism are former Fundamentalists who have been deeply hurt by their experiences in Fundamentalism. Along with their pain, they may also feel anger toward Fundamentalism. This is certainly understandable; it is natural to be angry with those who hurt us.

Tragically, some people, while attempting to escape the pain they felt when they were Fundamentalists, have given up their Christian faith. We feel deep regret that people have experienced such pain and equally deep regret that they have lost their Christian faith. Naturally, we would like to be helpful to them.

Still, our purpose in this book is not to address special concerns like these. Other people are making efforts to address those concerns, and we want to mention two books we have found especially helpful. *Growing Pains* by Randall Balmer[5] and *Soul Survivor* by Philip Yancey[6] are moving accounts of two thoughtful Christians' exodus from Fundamentalism. These books are particularly helpful because the authors have refused to become embittered by their experiences, and they have not left the Christian faith, though they have left the Fundamentalist version of it. We believe these books will be helpful to people who have been hurt by Fundamentalism but want to maintain their personal commitment to the Christian faith.

We have also not written our book for people who want to read an academic monograph on Fundamentalism. The scholarly literature on Fundamentalism is vast and growing, and we have been helped by the work of scholars who have studied Fundamentalism. Among the academic books we have found especially helpful are Nancy Ammerman's *Bible Believers*,[7] Ernest Sandeen's *The Roots of Fundamentalism*,[8] George Marsden's *Fundamentalism and American Culture*,[9] Joel Carpenter's *Revive Us Again*,[10] and a five-volume set titled *The Fundamentalism Project*, edited by Martin Marty and Scott Appleby.[11] Naturally we have done our best to insure that what we have written is as accurate as possible; that is one reason we have studied books such as these. However, we have not attempted to write as neutral observers but as Christian ministers attempting to be of service to non-Fundamentalist Christians in the United States.

We have written our book for non-Fundamentalist Christians of any denomination. However, we will devote the final two chapters and the conclusion of our book to the special concerns of readers who want to understand the relationship between Fundamentalism and progressive Baptists; we think, however, that those chapters contain principles that are transferable to Christians of all denominations.

Our Objectives

Our first objective is to provide an interpretation of Fundamentalism that will help our readers understand the Fundamentalist impulse and the Fundamentalist movement. Some readers may be baffled about the attraction Fundamentalism has for so many people. If our readers have found Fundamentalism puzzling, we hope to provide clarity. If they have encountered atypical expressions of Fundamentalism, we hope to provide a fuller and more balanced understanding.

We think modern Christians need an informed understanding of Fundamentalism. In the United States today, Fundamentalism is a prominent factor in the society in which we all live and work, so it seems reasonable to assume that we will be able to live more faithfully and work more productively if we understand it than if we do not.

Our second objective is to help people who are presently engaged in the process of considering whether they should be Fundamentalists; our message to them is that Fundamentalism is not the only authentic expression of Christian faith. We recognize that the stark choice "either Fundamentalism or secularism" has a certain plausibility to people today. We hope to show that in the end there are other alternatives.

Our third objective is that our readers will understand Fundamentalism well enough to be empowered to relate to Fundamentalists in a healthy way. Nothing would please us more than to know that some of our readers came to recognize the humanity of Fundamentalists and then decided to build bridges of understanding to Fundamentalists in their families, churches, or communities.

Our Plan

Our plan for this book is as follows: First, we will give attention to the ways in which the word *fundamentalism* is now used to describe movements in non-Christian religions. Throughout this book we will follow the practice of Grant Wacker and others of writing *Fundamentalism* (capitalized) when we specifically refer to the original Christian movement and *fundamentalism* (lowercased) when we refer to larger, more general movements which include other religions such as Islam or Judaism.[12]

In chapter 2, we will describe the original, American, Protestant version of Fundamentalism. In chapter 3 we will give attention to the theology of Fundamentalism, a subject dear to the hearts of Fundamentalists and of ourselves. We will devote chapter 4 to attitudes associated with Fundamentalism.

In chapter 5, we will review the relationships between Fundamentalism and Southern Baptists, and in the final chapter we will offer suggestions about how non-Fundamentalist Christians may relate to Fundamentalists.

The Authors

One of us (Philip) is a pastor, and the other (Fisher) is a professor in a divinity school. We have been friends for a third of a century. Neither of us is a Fundamentalist. Both of us experienced Fundamentalism firsthand when we were teenagers; some of our experiences were positive, and some were negative. Both of us today have friends who are Fundamentalists. We think of ourselves as traditional Christians and as traditional Baptists rather than as Fundamentalists.

We cheerfully acknowledge that, as traditional Christians and traditional Baptists, we hold many beliefs and practices in common with Fundamentalists, and we believe these include some of our most important beliefs and practices. Even so, for most Christians, perhaps for all, there are ways of following Jesus Christ that we believe are more faithful to Christ than the ways of Fundamentalism, and in our book we will attempt to say what those are and why we think they are more faithful.[13]

NOTES

[1] Since the conference, Dr. Bauder has become president of his seminary.

[2] Karen Armstrong, *The Battle for God* (New York: Alfred A. Knopf, 2001), ix.

[3] Barbara Kingsolver, *The Poisonwood Bible* (New York: HarperFlamingo, 1998).

[4] Margaret Atwood, *The Handmaid's Tale* (Boston: Houghton Mifflin, 1986).

[5] Randall Balmer, *Growing Pains: Learning to Love My Father's Faith* (Grand Rapids: Brazos Press, 2001).

[6] Philip Yancey, *Soul Survivor: How My Faith Survived the Church* (New York: Doubleday, 2001).

[7] Nancy Tatom Ammerman, *Bible Believers: Fundamentalists in the Modern World* (New Brunswick: Rutgers University Press, 1987).

[8] Ernest R. Sandeen, *The Roots of Fundamentalism: British and American Millenarianism, 1800–1930* (Chicago: The University of Chicago Press, 1970).

[9] George Marsden, *Fundamentalism and American Culture: The Shaping of Twentieth-century Evangelicalism, 1870–1925* (Oxford: Oxford University Press, 1980).

[10] Joel A. Carpenter, *Revive Us Again: The Reawakening of American Fundamentalism* (New York: Oxford University Press, 1997).

[11] Martin E. Marty and R. Scott Appleby, eds., *The Fundamentalism Project* (Chicago: The University of Chicago Press, 1991–1995).

[12] See Grant Wacker, "The Rise of Fundamentalism," on the website of the National Humanities Center: <http://www.nhc.rtp.nc.us/tserve/twenty/tkeyinfo/fundam.htm>.

[13] Though we are not sure, we think it is possible that for some people, the only possible expression of Christian faith and commitment is the Fundamentalist expression.

CHAPTER 1

GENERIC FUNDAMENTALISM

For at least a quarter of a century, perhaps longer, many religious commentators have referred to certain people in the different religions of the world as fundamentalists. For example, some news reporters described the terrorists who attacked the World Trade Center and the Pentagon on September 11, 2001, as "Islamic fundamentalists."

The association of the word *fundamentalist* with violence and terrorism is becoming so close that Bob Jones III, the president of Bob Jones University, has announced that he will no longer refer to himself and his colleagues as *Fundamentalists*, even though they have proudly called themselves by that name for more than half a century.[1] If this trend continues, there could come a time when few people are willing to describe themselves as fundamentalists.

Scholars have a different problem with the generic use of the word *fundamentalism*. They are concerned about its vagueness. Martin Marty and Scott Appleby have considered this issue carefully.[2] They reviewed other possible terms, but they retained *fundamentalism* because a word is needed, this one is already widely used, and no other word is better.

They are right; a term is needed to describe the religious tendency or impulse that movements in the different religions have in common. As Marty and Appleby have said, there is a family resemblance between movements in the various religions, and seeing that family resemblance is an indispensable step in understanding the movements themselves. The family resemblance includes several factors; Marty and Appleby have described these, and we will now review some of their findings.[3]

Religious Origins

One common factor is that each of the forms of fundamentalism originated in a religion. There are fundamentalist movements not only in Protestantism but also in Catholicism, Judaism, Islam, Hinduism, Buddhism, Sikhism, Confucianism, and other religions. In principle it might be possible to refer to a fundamentalist impulse and movement in a nonreligious ideology such as Marxism, but that usage is rare. Fundamentalism is a religious impulse that drives a religious movement, and any interpretation of fundamentalism that does not include an account of its religious character is to that extent incomplete and misleading.

A Selective Use of Tradition

A second factor is that fundamentalists are traditionalists who are selective about the aspects of their tradition that they retain. They do not retain everything. For example, the Hebrew Scriptures describe a world in which slavery, polygamy, and patriarchy were all practiced routinely; Jewish fundamentalists today retain patriarchy but not slavery or polygamy.

Because fundamentalists are selective in what they retain from their religious tradition, they sometimes find themselves in situations where their opponents are more traditional than the fundamentalists are on a particular issue. We will illustrate this point later in the book.

To understand fundamentalists well, one needs to recognize that their use of their religious tradition is selective rather than comprehensive.

The Modern World

A third family trait shared by all the varieties of fundamentalism is that they react against aspects of the modern world. Where there is no reaction against modernity, there is no fundamentalism. This means fundamentalism did not come into existence until the rise of modernity. There have been many religious traditionalists who were not fundamentalists because they lived before there was a modern world against which to react.

Fundamentalists do not reject everything about the modern world. They are selective about what they reject and what they accept. For example, some Islamic fundamentalists use a modern means of communication, the World Wide Web, to campaign against a modern idea, namely, that women should participate in public life as fully as men do. Interpretations of fundamentalism should include accounts of the aspects of modernity against which fundamentalists are reacting and how they express that reaction.

Under Siege

A fourth factor in fundamentalism is that fundamentalists reject aspects of the modern world for a definite reason, namely, that they perceive the modern world as a threat to their personal and corporate identity. Fundamentalists believe their faith and their community are under siege from aspects of modernity. They understand themselves to be protecting their religious faith and way of life from what Walter Lippman called "the acids of modernity."[4]

One of the ways those of us who are not fundamentalists can develop sympathy for fundamentalists is to recognize that they are doing what they are doing because they feel threatened by aspects of the modern world. An interpretation of fundamentalism that fails to offer an account of the threat fundamentalists feel is to that extent incomplete.

Militancy

A fifth family trait of fundamentalism is that fundamentalists react to modernity by fighting against it. There are, of course, other ways for traditionalists in the various religions to relate to modernity. For example, they can ignore it, or they can withdraw from modern society as the Amish do. Fundamentalists neither ignore modernity nor withdraw from it; they think choosing these responses to modernity is betraying their religious faith. They fight modernity, and they believe they are fighting for their religious lives.

Sometimes fundamentalists demonize their enemies. It is easy to assume that, when you believe an idea deeply and explain it clearly, anyone who does not agree with you is either ignorant or evil. However, many modern people have come to believe that it is a sign of maturity to accept the fact that intelligent, decent people sincerely disagree with your own carefully thought-out ideas.

Many fundamentalists reject this understanding of maturity. They feel, quite simply, that their unbelieving enemies are evil. For some fundamentalists, this constitutes a justification of their acting with violence against their enemies. Fortunately, this usually does not happen, but if we are to understand it when it does happen, we need to recognize that many fundamentalists sincerely believe that those who are not on their side are in fact evil.

Authoritarian Male Leaders

A sixth factor is that authoritarian males lead fundamentalist movements. Appleby and Marty wrote, "In the process of interpreting the tradition, evaluating modernity, and selectively retrieving salient elements of both, *charismatic and authoritarian male leaders* play a central role."[5]

A View of History

A seventh factor is that fundamentalism includes a view of history. Fundamentalists remember the past as better than the present. They see the present as bad and getting worse; in fact, they frequently see the present as a time of crisis. They look to a future when, they believe, their tradition will be victorious. In their view of history, fundamentalists usually decline to employ the category of progress which plays such an important role in conventional modern views of history.

Definite Boundaries

An eighth factor in fundamentalism is that fundamentalists distinguish carefully between true believers and others; they draw clear, definite lines between insiders and outsiders, and they keep the outsiders outside.

It is not unusual for fundamentalists to take extreme steps that effectively separate true believers from everyone else. As they embrace ideas and practices that many of their modern or even traditional fellow religionists find scandalous, they make clear who the real believers are.

The extreme steps fundamentalists take often puzzle outsiders. In fact, however, it makes perfect sense if one bears in mind that fundamentalists believe the following: first, history is a conflict between good and evil; second, aspects of modernity threaten the identity and existence of the community of true faith; third, the community is fighting for its life against the modern world. Given those beliefs, it is reasonable to take extreme steps as a way of drawing a line in the sand and thereby making clear who the insiders and outsiders are, because in so doing the community will have a chance of surviving the threat modernity poses to its existence.

In addition to distinguishing themselves from their enemies, fundamentalists are careful not to become contaminated by contact with their enemies. This is also a part of the process of achieving an identity for their community.

A Totalitarian Impulse

Ninth and finally, fundamentalists have as their goal replacing modernity with their own religious system. They do not work toward coexistence with those whom they see as their enemies, but toward control of their society. Marty and Appleby refer to this as the *totalitarian impulse* in fundamentalism.[6] It reinforces the determination of fundamentalists to avoid cooperation with non-fundamentalists.

Conclusion

At the end of the first volume of *The Fundamentalism Project*, Marty and Appleby wrote:

> In these pages, then, fundamentalism has appeared as a tendency, a habit of mind, found within religious communities and paradigmatically embodied in certain representative individuals and movements, which manifests itself as a strategy, or set of strategies, by which beleaguered believers attempt to preserve their distinctive identity as a people or group. Finding this identity to be at risk in the contemporary era, they fortify it by a selective retrieval of doctrines, beliefs, and practices from a sacred past.[7]

This is a useful summary of some of the factors that together constitute the family resemblance between the fundamentalist movements in the various religions and that therefore justify the use of the word *fundamentalists* to describe people in these numerous, diverse movements.

We turn our attention now to the original Fundamentalism.

NOTES

[1] See Bob Jones's article regarding the term's usage, published in the President's Column, *BJU Review*, Spring, 2002:<http://www.bju.edu/aboutbju/pca/spring02>.

[2] Martin Marty and Scott Appleby, *Fundamentalisms Observed*, vol. 1 of *The Fundamentalism Project* (Chicago: The University of Chicago Press, 1991), vii-xiii.

[3] Marty and Appleby, *Fundamentalisms Observed*, ch. 15. We have rearranged and reworded some but not all of their findings.

[4] Walter Lippman, *A Preface to Morals* (New York: The Macmillan Company, 1929), ch. 4.

[5] Appleby and Marty, *Fundamentalisms Observed*, 826.

[6] Ibid., 834.

[7] Ibid., 835. This important chapter contains other ideas that we decided not to incorporate into our description.

CHAPTER 2

THE ORIGINAL FUNDAMENTALISM

Background

Fundamentalism began among Protestants in America. In the nineteenth century, the dominant religion in America was Christianity, the dominant form of Christianity was Protestantism, and the dominant type of Protestantism was evangelicalism, which emphasized that every person needs to be converted and that evangelism is a principal mission of the church.

Throughout the nineteenth century, American churches expended a lot of energy on denominational polemics, arguing that "ours is the true church and yours isn't," and so on. Even though the evangelical Protestants in America weren't exactly united and of course had no official governmental support, evangelicalism exercised a cultural hegemony in America.

Four Enemies

Four new sets of ideas changed this situation. They were the Enlightenment, biblical criticism, biological evolution, and liberal theology.

The Enlightenment

The Enlightenment was a prominent stream of thought in Europe and the English colonies beginning in the eighteenth century. Four ideas characteristic of the Enlightenment were individualism, reason, freedom, and progress.[1] Enlightenment thinkers tended to have confidence that the principal human problems could be solved if human beings would set aside their prejudices and superstitions and think rationally about their world. They also believed progress toward that bright future depended upon individuals being set free from all tyrannies, which in practice meant the authoritarian state and the authoritarian church. Politically, the Enlightenment commitment to freedom led to the American and French revolutions and to modern liberal democracy; Benjamin Franklin and Thomas Jefferson were respected Enlightenment thinkers. Religiously, the commitment to freedom constituted a challenge to the authority of the churches; frequently this took the form of individuals doubting discrete beliefs of the Christian faith. Jefferson, for example, retained a strong belief in God, morality, and immortality, but he was dismissive of much of the rest of traditional Christian belief.[2]

Biblical Criticism

The Enlightenment gave rise to, among other things, biblical criticism.[3] Biblical criticism is a way of studying the Bible that takes seriously the Bible's historical character; indeed, it sometimes is called the historical-critical study of the Bible.

Christians have never claimed that the Bible was dropped down from heaven; they have always recognized that human beings such as David and Isaiah, Paul and John wrote it. They have believed God inspired the writers of the Bible so that what they wrote is the Word of God as well as the words of human beings, but they have never denied that human beings wrote the Bible.

However, Christian churches have not always been attentive to the historical character of the origin of the Bible, so when biblical criticism arose, with its heightened attentiveness to the historical setting of the human writers, it was an unfamiliar method of studying the Bible. In addition, it was characteristic of critical scholars that they did not simply report what the authors of the Bible had written, but they formulated their own questions and then ransacked the Bible and other sources for answers. Here is how one scholar expressed this: "The scissors-and-paste historian reads [sources] in a simply receptive spirit, to find out what they said. The scientific historian reads them with a question in his mind, having taken the initiative by deciding for himself what he wants to find out from them."[4]

As might be expected, the scholars who employed this new method of Bible study sometimes arrived at conclusions concerning the message of the Bible that were not only unfamiliar to Christians but were at variance with what Christians had believed for centuries. Naturally this was threatening to some Christians, so many of them resisted it. This continues to be the case today.

Evolution

It is possible to give an exact date for the beginnings of the impact of the idea of biological evolution upon Christian faith. Charles Darwin's book *The Origin of Species* was published in 1859, and from that year until the present there has been a continuing controversy in some churches concerning biological evolution.

The basic idea behind biological evolution is that all of the varied life forms on Earth today, including human beings, have evolved over a vast period of time from simpler life forms. This means human beings emerged relatively recently from lower forms of ancestors.

Darwin's particular proposal undermined an ancient and popular argument for the existence of God known as the teleological argument. The Greek word *telos* means *design*. Things in nature appear to have been designed: eyes seemed to have been designed for seeing, hands for grasping, and so on. The teleological argument is that, if there is design, there has to be a Designer, and that is God.

Darwin proposed an alternative explanation for apparent design in the world, an explanation that eliminated the need for a Designer. The seemingly designed factors, he said, are the product of mutations that occur randomly from one generation to the next and that happen to equip some organisms to survive and procreate better than others. These random mutations seem to have been designed, but in fact they are accidental rather than designed. Darwin's proposal seemed to many Christians to deal a crushing blow to the argument for God from apparent design in the world.

In addition to undermining this popular argument for the existence of God, evolution put two other Christian beliefs at risk. Since it suggested that human beings share common ancestors with other creatures, it undermined the belief that human beings are special creations of God, as the Bible teaches. Also, evolution undermined confidence in the trustworthiness of the accounts of creation found in Genesis and elsewhere in the Bible that, of course, say nothing about evolution.

Liberal Theology

Liberal theology was the work of academic theologians who attempted to incorporate into their thinking about God insights from the Enlightenment, biblical criticism, and biological evolution. Liberal theology took a great many forms; what these forms had in common was an interpretation of the Christian faith that their authors believed were resistant to the acids of modernity derived from the Enlightenment and found in biblical criticism and biological evolution.

Among scholars it has been traditional to use the word *modernism* when these ideas appeared in the Roman Catholic Church and the word *liberalism* when the ideas appeared in Protestant churches. Because these differences are not important for our purposes in this book, and because the word *modernism* is not widely used today, we shall use the word *liberalism* for these ideas wherever they may have appeared.

Responding to the Enemies

Clergy and laypeople in American churches encountered the Enlightenment, biblical criticism, evolutionary theory, and liberal theology slowly and piecemeal, but by the beginning of the twentieth century large numbers of them had come to believe that these new ideas constituted the thin edge of a wedge that would lead inevitably to secularism and therefore to unbelief.

People use the word *secularism* in a wide range of ways. For example, sometimes it is said that a college has become secular if in the past it always had clergymen as presidents and it now has a layperson as president; that is a minimalist understanding of secularism. Maximally, secularism is an understanding of all of reality in which it is asserted that there is no sacred reality transcending the world we experience through our senses (the Latin word for the nonsacred world is *sæculum*); in other words, secularism is atheism. This is how we will use the word in this book.

Once people began to interpret liberalism as a secularizing force threatening the Christian faith, there were various ways they could oppose it. One was to write scholarly books challenging it. European theologians such as Albert Schweitzer and Karl Barth did this. Albert Schweitzer's book *The Quest of the Historical Jesus* subverted one of the most impressive and characteristic productions of liberal theology, namely, the biographies of Jesus. Liberal theologians had written many dozens of critical studies of the life of Jesus during the nineteenth century, and some of them had been widely read. In the forceful conclusion to his book Schweitzer wrote:

> There is nothing more negative than the result of the critical study of the Life of Jesus. The Jesus of Nazareth who came forward publicly as the Messiah, who preached the ethic of the Kingdom of God, who founded the Kingdom of Heaven upon earth, and died to give His work its final consecration, never had any existence. He is a figure designed by rationalism, endowed with life by liberalism, and clothed by modern theology in an historical garb.
>
> It is a good thing that the true historical Jesus should overthrow the modern Jesus, should rise up against the modern spirit and send upon earth, not peace, but a sword. He was not a teacher, not a casuist; He was an imperious ruler . . . . He comes to us as One unknown, without a name, as of old, by the lake-side, He came to those men who knew Him not. He speaks to us the same word: "Follow thou me!" and sets us to the tasks which He has to fulfill for our time. He commands. And to those who obey Him, whether they be wise or simple, He will reveal Himself in the toils, the conflicts, the sufferings which they shall pass through in His fellowship, and, as an ineffable mystery, they shall learn in their own experience Who He is.[5]

Schweitzer's book was published in German in 1906 and in English in 1910. A few years later a Swiss theologian and pastor named Karl Barth began to challenge the dominant liberal theology in which he had been educated. In a 1916 address titled "The Strange New World within the Bible," Barth argued that the Bible is not really a book of history or of morals or even of religion, in the sense of how human beings are supposed to act. It is rather a book of God:

> It is not the right human thoughts about God which form the content of the Bible, but the right divine thoughts about men. The Bible tells us not how we should talk with God but what he says to us; not how we find the way to him, but how he has sought and found the way to us; not the right relation in which we must place ourselves to him, but the covenant which he has made with all who are Abraham's spiritual children and which he has sealed once and for all in Jesus Christ. It is this which is within the Bible. The word of God is within the Bible.
>
> Our grandfathers, after all, were right when they struggled so desperately in behalf of the truth that there is revelation in the Bible and not religion only, and when they would not allow facts to be turned upside down for them even by so pious and intelligent a man as Schleiermacher.[6]

Schweitzer and Barth represented characteristic forms of European resistance to aspects of liberal theology, and they showed that a theological response to liberalism could be effective. Schweitzer became a missionary and one of the most admired men of the twentieth century. Barth went on to become the most influential Christian theologian of the twentieth century, and today, almost a century later, his influence is still great. These men changed the course of Christian theology in the twentieth century by showing the defects in some liberal theology.

Another way to oppose liberalism was to organize, and that happened in America. Large numbers of Protestants set aside their denominational differences in order to form a loose coalition to oppose liberalism. That coalition came to be known as the Fundamentalist movement.

In summary, the original Fundamentalism was a movement of traditional Protestants in the United States who set aside their denominational differences in order to form a united front against a common enemy, liberalism, which they understood to be the thin edge of the wedge of secularism and a serious threat to the faith of the Christian church. Fundamentalism began as a religious impulse to protect traditional beliefs by opposing liberalism, the impulse led to a movement, and the movement created a network of institutions that embodied the impulse.

If the interpretation of liberalism as inevitably leading to secularism were true, then anyone, including Fundamentalists, who resisted liberalism would have been right to think that their fight against liberalism was a fight for the survival of the Christian faith, since the Christian faith is, of course, a religious rather than a secular view of life.

There is an irony in the Fundamentalists' assumption that liberal theology would lead inevitably to unbelief. Liberal theologians had accommodated changes brought on by modernity for the precise purpose of helping modern people retain their Christian faith, but the Fundamentalists came to think of liberal theology itself as a threat to Christian faith, indeed, as the principal threat to the faith.

So they committed themselves to fight liberalism. George W. Dollar, who is a Fundamentalist and a historian of the original

Fundamentalism, has proposed the following definition of *Fundamentalism*: "Historic Fundamentalism is the literal exposition of all the affirmations and attitudes of the Bible and the militant exposure of all non-Biblical affirmations and attitudes."[7] He was equally emphatic about the militancy of Fundamentalism in a second volume that he "Dedicated to *FIGHTING FUNDAMEN-TALISTS: Stand . . . Stand . . . Stand (Ephesians 5:11-14)*."[8]

Bob Jones III, a contemporary Fundamentalist leader, emphasized the need for militancy in defending the faith in the following statement:

> A genuine Fundamentalist is a man who does four things: First, he believes the Bible—accepts it without question as the divinely, verbally inspired, authoritative, and inerrant Word of God. Second, he defends the Word of God without equivocation, hesitation, or apology. He does battle for the Faith. In the third place, a Fundamentalist declares the whole counsel of God. He does not say with Billy Graham, "God has called me only to preach the gospel." He recognizes the fact that the same Book that says, "preach the gospel," says, "Preach the word . . . reprove, rebuke, exhort with all longsuffering and doctrine." He does everything that God requires of a good servant who, as Paul reminded Timothy, will put the brethren in remembrance that certain apostates and false teachers will arise in the last days. He rebukes unscriptural attitudes, actions, and alliances. Fourth, a Fundamentalist obeys the Scripture, seeking in every point to confirm not only by his way of life but also by his own alliances, affiliations, and connections, his belief in the inerrancy of the Word of God. To be a Fundamentalist one must be a complete separatist, fully in compliance with scriptural standards, and an example of obedience to the commands of God.[9]

Believe the Bible, defend the Bible, rebuke those who do not believe the Bible, and separate from those who do not believe the Bible. Fighting for the faith is an essential component of Fundamentalism.

The Name *Fundamentalism*

The name *Fundamentalism* is associated with two events. One is the publication of a series of twelve pamphlets containing ninety articles; these were published between 1910 and 1915 with the title *The Fundamentals.* Two California businessmen, Lyman and Milton Stewart, arranged for about three million copies of *The Fundamentals* to be distributed free to Christian leaders in America and abroad. In an introduction to a facsimile edition of *The Fundamentals*, historian George Marsden wrote that "*The Fundamentals* may have been quite literally the first shot in the fundamentalist controversies."[10]

The second event associated with the word *Fundamentalists* occurred five years later. On July 1, 1920, a Northern Baptist newspaper editor named Curtis Lee Laws wrote a column in which he said:

> We here and now move that a new word be adopted to describe the men among us who insist that the landmarks shall not be removed. . . . We suggest that those who still cling to the great fundamentals and who mean to do battle royal for the fundamentals shall be called "Fundamentalists." By that name the editor of *The Watchman-Examiner* is willing to be called. It will be understood therefore when he uses the word it will be in compliment and not in disparagement.[11]

Soon the words *Fundamentalism* and *Fundamentalist* became standard for designating the movement and its members. Initially they were not regarded as pejorative words; many people happily thought of themselves as Fundamentalists, just as Laws had done.

The Center of Gravity

For a long time the conventional wisdom was that Fundamentalism was a Southern, rural, anti-intellectual movement. In fact, the original movement was stronger in the North than in the South, probably because at the time so few Southerners felt threatened by liberalism; it was more urban than rural, and originally its leaders included intellectuals such as J. Gresham Machen.[12]

Initially the two denominations most affected by Fundamentalism were the Northern Baptist Convention and the Northern Presbyterians (UPCUSA). Fundamentalists attempted to take control of these denominations, and, when they failed, many of them separated from the denominations, characterizing them as apostate. Apostasy is an intentional abandonment of the Christian faith by people who once held it; an individual who unintentionally embraces erroneous views is not an apostate. Because Fundamentalists believed these two denominations to be apostate, they felt obligated to separate from them. The practice of separation became a prominent characteristic of some Fundamentalists, and across the years they developed precise understandings of various types of separation and the justifications for them.

A Loose Coalition

Fundamentalism was a loose coalition, and this has two implications. The first is that no one in the movement had the authority to draw up a definitive list of the fundamentals. As we shall see in the next chapter, this makes it difficult to be accurate when attempting to offer general statements about Fundamentalist theology.

The other implication is that there were differences among people in the movement. It is worth taking a moment to consider examples of these differences.

A major emphasis in the original Fundamentalism was an appeal to inerrant original manuscripts of the Bible as a defense against biblical criticism. Princeton theologians such as B. B. Warfield had developed this strategy. However, James Orr, who wrote the first article in *The Fundamentals*, rejected inerrancy.

A second major emphasis in the original Fundamentalism was dispensational premillennialism. This is a particular understanding about a series of events that, premillennialists believe, will occur at the end of the world, and it frequently includes the idea that the end of the world is near. Yet the Princeton theologians such as Warfield who gave to Fundamentalism its understanding of biblical inerrancy were opponents of premillennialism.

Another emphasis in the original Fundamentalism was a form of holiness pietism known as *the deeper life* and associated with the evangelist D. L. Moody and the Bible conference movement in America and with the Keswick Movement in England. While many Fundamentalists embraced this understanding of Christian living, other Fundamentalists such as the Princeton theologians rejected the theology of the deeper life as a form of perfectionism.[13]

In summary, Fundamentalism was a coalition of people who had considerable theological as well as denominational differences, and this makes it difficult to achieve precision about the theology of Fundamentalism.

Stages of Development

As we have seen, Fundamentalists began with a sense of entitlement to exercise hegemony in American life. We think, to the extent that they represented traditional, Protestant, evangelical Christianity, they were right to claim that historically their expression of Christianity was the majority view in America. Then, beginning during the 1920s, Fundamentalism engaged in some of its greatest battles[14] and suffered a series of major defeats. The principal defeat was that Fundamentalists failed to take control of any denomination, though they made sustained efforts to do so.

The Scopes trial in Dayton, Tennessee, was another major defeat for Fundamentalism.[15] In March 1925, the legislature of Tennessee passed a law prohibiting the teaching of evolution in public schools. John Scopes, a teacher in a public high school, acting on behalf of the then five-year-old American Civil Liberties Union, tested the law by teaching evolution, and he was brought to trial in summer 1925. He was defended by one of America's ablest and most famous trial lawyers, Clarence Darrow. The prosecuting attorneys were assisted by one of the best-known Fundamentalist leaders, William Jennings Bryan. The Democratic Party had nominated Bryan for President of the United States on three different occasions, he had served as Secretary of State under Woodrow Wilson, and he was one of the most famous orators in America.

The trial was broadcast on radio; it was one of the first public events broadcast around the country through an ad hoc network of stations. Among the reporters present for the trial was H. L. Mencken, who wrote, among many other caustic things, that Tennessee was a sort of holy land for imbeciles.

Fundamentalists won the battle in Dayton, but they lost the war. Scopes was found guilty and fined, but public opinion began to turn against Fundamentalism.

A third defeat for Fundamentalism was the repeal early in the administration of Franklin D. Roosevelt of the amendment to the Constitution prohibiting the sale of alcoholic beverages. Fundamentalists had worked hard to get the Eighteenth

Amendment passed in 1919, and it was a severe setback to them when that amendment was repealed in 1933.

The character of Fundamentalism's leadership began to shift in the 1930s, passing from scholars such as J. Gresham Machen to Bible teachers and evangelists such as Bob Jones and John R. Rice.

During the 1930s, the movement more or less disappeared from public view, and many Americans assumed that, except for a few benighted people in isolated locales, it had died. In the introduction to his book on Fundamentalism, historian Ernest Sandeen made a witty comment about this: "This book is not the obituary of Fundamentalism. Ever since its rise to notoriety in the 1920s, scholars have predicted the imminent demise of the movement. The Fundamentalists, to return the favor, have predicted the speedy end of the world."[16] In fact, of course, Fundamentalism had not died, but rather was flourishing. Its proponents continued to disseminate their views, some of them working within the traditional Protestant denominations and others creating an enormous network and a subculture of their own outside the denominations.

In the following decades, the achievements of those who remained more or less independent of the older denominations were impressive. They made effective use of radio. They conducted many productive evangelistic campaigns, large and small, throughout the nation. They founded and built numerous independent churches, some of which became enormous. They operated dozens of institutions of higher education, including Bible institutes, colleges, and seminaries. They sent tens of thousands of people to serve as missionaries abroad. In terms both of their numbers and their activities, they were a major expression of Christianity in America, a fact that sometimes has been overlooked by those who write about this part of the history of American Christianity.

During this period many Fundamentalists gave careful attention to the matter of separation. Some of them called for strict separation from all non-Fundamentalists and also from Fundamentalists who had not separated from all non-Fundamentalists, but others called for holding on to the fundamentals and battling liberalism while remaining within the denominations.[17]

In the 1940s Fundamentalism gave birth to a friendlier, more open movement that today is known as evangelicalism and is best represented by Billy Graham. The exact relationship between Fundamentalism and post-Fundamentalist evangelicalism has been studied at length by historians and by theologians.[18] Like Fundamentalists, evangelicals affirmed the fundamentals of the Christian faith and saw in liberalism a concealed secularism that threatened the church's faith and life. The important question was, "Are the two really different, or are evangelicals just Fundamentalists with good manners," as one theologian put it?[19]

Two differences between Fundamentalism and evangelicalism suggest to us that they are significantly dissimilar. One is that evangelicals intentionally resisted the anti-intellectualism that came to characterize large sectors of Fundamentalism beginning in the 1930s, and the other is that evangelicals were willing to cooperate with Christians from whom Fundamentalists felt obliged to separate. Both of these differences are evident in a comment criticizing evangelicals made by the Fundamentalist leader Bob Jones: "An evangelical is someone who says to a liberal, 'I'll call you a Christian, if you'll call me a scholar.'"[20]

In the late 1970s Fundamentalism reemerged as a political power in American life in the work of Jerry Falwell and the Moral Majority.[21] Today it remains an influential movement in the American churches and in American public life.

It does so despite the fact that, when non-Fundamentalists talk about Fundamentalism, they usually are much clearer about what they think is wrong with it than about the positive message and contributions of the movement. It is debatable whether that is the fault of the Fundamentalists or of their critics, but in any case it is unusual to see a non-Fundamentalist who pays close attention to the movement, addresses it with respect, appreciates things in it, and yet remains a non-Fundamentalist. One contemporary Christian leader who has done this well is Richard John Neuhaus, formerly a Lutheran and now a Roman Catholic, who has written with wit and wisdom about Fundamentalists:

> The activist Fundamentalists want us to know that they are not going to go back to the wilderness. Many of them, being typical Americans, also want to be loved. . . . The country cousins have shown up in force at the family picnic. They want a few rules changed right away. Other than that they promise to behave, provided we do not again try to exclude them from family deliberations.[22]

It seems likely to us that Fundamentalism will remain an important part of American life for the foreseeable future. We know of no convincing reason to suppose that it is going to disappear.[23] It is a vigorous movement with a network of effective institutional support and a history of achievement in areas such as Christian missions, and its message clearly appeals to many people today.

However, though it seems likely that Fundamentalism will endure, it is unlikely that it will ever dominate American life. America probably will remain religiously pluralistic, with no one religious group having cultural dominance. We are all minorities now.

NOTES

[1] A classic statement about the Enlightenment is that of Immanuel Kant—"What Is Enlightenment?"—which may be seen at <http://eserver.org/philosophy/kant/what-is-enlightenment.txt>.

[2] Edwin S. Gaustad, *Sworn on the Altar of God: A Religious Biography of Thomas Jefferson* (Grand Rapids: William B. Eerdmans Publishing Company, 1996).

[3] F. L. Cross, ed., *The Oxford Dictionary of the Christian Church* (London: Oxford University Press, 1958), s. v. *Aufklärung*.

[4] R. G. Collingwood, *The Idea of History* (United States: Oxford Galaxy Book, 1961), 269.

[5] Albert Schweitzer, *The Quest of the Historical Jesus*, trans. W. Montgomery (New York: The Macmillan Company, 1961), 398, 403.

[6] Karl Barth, *The Word of God and the Word of Man*, trans. Douglas Horton (New York: Harper & Row, Publishers, 1957), 43-44.

[7] George W. Dollar, *A History of Fundamentalism in America* (Greenville SC: Bob Jones University Press, 1973), xv.

[8] George W. Dollar, *The Fight for Fundamentalism: American Fundamentalism, 1973–1983* (Sarasota FL: self-published, 1983), no page number.

[9] Bob Jones III, "Pseudo-Fundamentalists: The New Breed in Sheep's Clothing." This statement is available online at <http://www.bju.edu/resources/faith/1978/issue1/pseudo.html>.

[10] George M. Marsden, ed., *The Fundamentals* (New York: Garland Publishing, Inc., 1988), I: no page number.

[11] Curtis Lee Laws, "Convention Side Lights," *The Watchman-Examiner* 8/27 (1 July 1920): 834.

[12] One catches a glimpse of how much respect even an agnostic intellectual such as Walter Lippman had for Machen in Lippman's *A Preface to Morals* (New York: The Macmillan Company, 1929), 30-35.

[13] George Marsden, *Fundamentalism and American Culture: The Shaping of Twentieth-century Evangelicalism, 1870–1925* (Oxford: Oxford University Press, 1980), 98.

[14] Bill Leonard has provided an especially helpful summary of the battles in the Baptist denominations in the United States. See Bill J. Leonard, *Baptist Ways: A History* (Valley Forge: Judson Press, 2003), 397-406.

[15] For overlooked information about the trial, see Carol Iannone, "The Truth about Inherit the Wind," *First Things* 70 (February 1997): 28-33; it is available at <http://www.firstthings.com/ftissues/ft9702/articles/iannone.html>.

[16] Ernest R. Sandeen, *The Roots of Fundamentalism: British and American Millenarianism, 1800–1930* (Chicago: The University of Chicago Press, 1970), ix.

[17] The most thoughtful account of Fundamentalist separatism during the era known to us is found in chs. 2–4 of Joel Carpenter, *Revive Us Again: The Reawakening of American Fundamentalism* (New York: Oxford University Press, 1997).

[18] Of many studies, we will mention three: George M. Marsden, *Reforming Fundamentalism: Fuller Seminary and the New Evangelicalism* (Grand Rapids: William B. Eerdmans Publishing Company, 1987); Carl F. H. Henry, *Confessions of a Theologian: An Autobiography* (Waco: Word Books, 1986); and William J. Abraham, *The Coming Great Revival: Recovering the Full Evangelical Tradition* (San Francisco: Harper Books, 1984).

[19] Abraham, *The Coming Great Revival,* ix.

[20] Bob Jones, Jr., *Corn Bread and Caviar* (Greenville: BJU Press, 1985), 104. Quoted in Carpenter, *Revive Us Again,* 241.

[21] Jerry Falwell, *Falwell: An Autobiography* (Lynchburg VA: Liberty House Publishers, 1997), ch. 14.

[22] Richard John Neuhaus, "What the Fundamentalists Want," in *Piety and Politics: Evangelicals and Fundamentalists Confront the World,* ed. Richard John Neuhaus and Michael Cromartie (Washington: Ethics and Public Policy Center, 1987), 18.

[23] Some non-Fundamentalists believe Fundamentalism will not survive long; one person who holds this view is Kirby Godsey; see <http://www.mercer.edu/baptiststudies/conferences/presentations/godsey.htm>.

CHAPTER 3

THE THEOLOGY OF FUNDAMENTALISM

Theology is important to Fundamentalists. In fact, it is not possible to understand Fundamentalism without understanding its theology.

Except for groups that formally adopt official creeds, it is difficult to pin down the precise theology of any religious movement, especially a coalition as loose as Fundamentalism. Inevitably, there are disagreements, if only minor ones, among members of any group. As we saw in the last chapter, this was true of the early Fundamentalists.

What we can do here is describe the theology displayed at particular moments in the history of Fundamentalism. For this purpose we have chosen two examples from the early history of Fundamentalism. The first is the series of pamphlets titled *The Fundamentals*; they display the theology of the Fundamentalist impulse before there was a Fundamentalist movement. The second is the Five Points of Fundamentalism; these were affirmed at the beginnings of the Fundamentalist movement.

The *Fundamentals*

The Fundamentals, the ninety tracts published from 1910 to 1915 and distributed to about three million people, represent a broad and generous Fundamentalism. Some of the articles were by traditional scholars such as James Orr of Scotland, B. B. Warfield of Princeton Theological Seminary, and E. Y. Mullins of the Southern Baptist Theological Seminary; others were by people associated with the new Bible schools such as the Moody Bible Institute of Chicago and the Bible Institute of Los Angeles. Perhaps because there was not yet an organized Fundamentalist movement when the pamphlets were published, the call to separate from denominations that include liberals is not prominent in *The Fundamentals*, as it would become in later years.

On the other hand, resistance to biblical criticism, evolution, and liberal theology—all understood to have secularizing tendencies—is evident in *The Fundamentals*. We shall review the articles found in the first volume and then, since none of these dealt directly with evolution, we shall look also at an article on that subject from volume 4.

The first article of volume 1 is by James Orr of Glasgow, and its subject is the virgin birth of Christ, a topic affirmed clearly in the Gospels of Matthew and Luke and treasured by Eastern Orthodox, Roman Catholic, and most Protestant Christians. Orr's objective was not so much to help his readers understand the virgin birth and its meaning as to defend the historicity of the virgin birth against those who had questioned or denied it. This is the opening sentence of his article, and therefore of *The Fundamentals*: "It is well known that the last ten or twenty years have been marked by a determined assault upon the truth of the Virgin birth of Christ."[1] In his article, Orr skillfully defended the fact of the virgin birth of Christ and also its religious importance, but he did not attempt to unpack the theological meaning of the virgin birth of Christ.

The second article was "The Deity of Christ" by Benjamin B. Warfield, and the author's purpose was identical to Orr's, namely, to defend the truth of his topic. He did this with great learning, drawing both upon individual passages of Scripture and also upon the impact Christ has made upon the world.[2]

In *The Fundamentals*, great prominence is given to Christ's deity, but little interest is shown in his humanity. So far as we can tell, the writers of *The Fundamentals* did not attempt to explore in a balanced way the Christian doctrine of the Incarnation, which says that in some wonderful and mysterious way Jesus was a single person who was both fully human and fully divine. The lack of attention to Jesus' humanity is serious, for if Jesus was not fully human, then, of course, there was no Incarnation.

If we ask why *The Fundamentals* do not contain a balanced emphasis on Jesus' humanity as well as his deity, the suggested answer is that the writers only addressed the subject they considered threatened in their time. The writers felt that virtually no one challenged Jesus' humanity but many challenged his divinity, so they addressed the latter subject and ignored the former.

This means they were doing polemics and apologetics, defending the faith from assaults from inside and outside the church, rather than theology, attempting to gain a better understanding of Christ. There is a place for polemics and apologetics in the church, but these activities tend not to yield a balanced, rounded view of the faith. Instead, they give an unbalanced one that reflects the struggles in which the authors are engaged.

The third article in the first volume is "The Purposes of the Incarnation" by G. Campbell Morgan, and, unlike the first two articles, this was not a defense of its subject. As the title suggests, it was instead an exploration of the reasons for the Incarnation. Morgan suggested there were four of these: to reveal God, to take away sins, to destroy the works of the devil, and to prepare people for a second coming.

The fourth article, "The Personality and Deity of the Holy Spirit," was by R. A. Torrey. Though the title suggests a broad treatment of the Spirit, the article is in fact a defense of the idea that the Spirit is a person rather than an impersonal power. Torrey simply appealed to numerous passages in the Bible in which it makes more sense to think of the Spirit in personal terms. This is an interesting article because, though it is polemical in character, it is not clear whom Torrey was opposing.[3]

The fifth article is titled "The Proof of the Living God," and in it the prayerful ministry of George Müller of Bristol is offered as evidence for the belief that God provides for those who genuinely trust God to do so. This is the first example in *The Fundamentals* of an interest in Christian experience, an interest represented repeatedly in later volumes as well. Even here, however, polemics was at work, for the author, A. T. Pierson, defended the idea that Müller was able to carry out his extraordinary ministries because of God's supernatural help and not, as some critics had alleged, by non-supernatural means. Pierson quoted a critic who said, "There was absolutely nothing in [Müller's] career which could not be accounted for as the result of purely natural causes."[4] In the article, Pierson repudiated such claims and issued "a challenge to unbelief" to attempt to do what Müller had done.[5]

The sixth article is titled "The History of the Higher Criticism,"[6] and in it Dyson Hague began by affirming the value of both Lower Criticism, in which efforts are made to determine which of the ancient manuscripts of the Bible has the text that is closest to the original, and a reverent Higher Criticism, in which are studied matters such as the date, authorship, and circumstances of the various books of the Bible. Next Hague offered an account of how Higher Criticism has become associated in people's minds with unbelief. In deciding on the authorship of books, its leaders depended too much on their own subjective judgments about writing styles; these leaders speculated too freely and fancifully about the Bible; and, "in the third place, the dominant men of the movement were men with a strong bias against the supernatural."[7] These critics, Hague said, did not do their work in order to help believers understand and appreciate the Bible or to confirm the reliability of the Scriptures "but to discredit in most cases their genuineness, to discover discrepancies, and throw doubt upon their authority."[8] "Another serious consequence of the Higher Critical movement is that it threatens the Christian system of doctrine and the whole fabric of systematic theology."[9] Hague did not think his opposition to irreverent biblical criticism made him an obscurantist; he welcomed all the light reverent criticism could throw upon the Scriptures. But he refused to be intimidated by the scholarship of critics who preferred to discredit the Bible rather than be loyal to Christ and his Church.[10]

The final article in volume 1 of *The Fundamentals* is a brief testimony by a Christian layman. Howard A. Kelly began by explaining that for twenty years he had accepted the criticism of the Old Testament without knowing how to reconcile this with his faith that the Bible is God's Word, but that one day he decided simply to believe about the Bible what the Bible says about itself. As a result, "I now believe the Bible to be the inspired Word of God, inspired in a sense utterly different from that of any merely human book," and "I believe Jesus Christ to be the Son of God."[11]

Because no article in volume 1 dealt with evolution, we will consider an article found in the fourth volume; it is by James Orr and is titled "Science and Christian Faith." In his introduction, Orr wrote that many people assume that science and religion are locked in combat and always have been, but in fact their assumption is mistaken. Historically the two disciplines have had friendly relations, and, apart from mistakes made by scientists and theologians, no conflict would occur between them.

In "Science and Law–Miracle," the first section of the article, Orr argued that miracle is essential for Christian faith and that the scientific emphasis on natural law has led many people to think miracle is no longer a credible idea. Orr said the Christian understanding of natural law is that it is God's creation and that God is free to act in the world:

> Just as, when I lift my arm, or throw a stone high in the air, I do not abolish the law of gravitation but counteract or overrule its purely natural action by the introduction of a new spiritual force; so, but in an infinitely higher way, is a miracle due to the interposition of the First Cause of all, God Himself. What the scientific man needs to establish his objection to miracle is, not simply that natural causes operate uniformly, but that no other than natural causes exist; that natural causes exhaust all the causation in the universe. And that, we hold, he can never do.[12]

Having dealt with the anti-supernaturalism issue, which is the principal source of Christians' reservations about science, Orr then turned to the individual sciences and their relationship to the Bible, giving special attention to the question of evolution. He rejected Darwin's proposals concerning natural selection, but he did so for scientific rather than religious reasons. Orr gently embraced the idea that human beings have evolved from lower forms of life, arguing that evolution was the form taken by God's creative work. He insisted that evolution must offer an account of new factors entering the process. Inorganic chemicals become organic with the entrance of life; living organisms become conscious beings with the entrance of consciousness; conscious beings become human beings with the entrance of rationality, personality, and moral life. The new facts in the process should be recognized as God's creative work: "'Evolution,' in short, is coming to be recognized as but a new name for 'creation,' only that the creative power now works from *within*, instead of, as in the old conception, in an *external*, plastic fashion. It is, however, creation none the less."[13] It is also evolution nonetheless. But it is not Darwinian evolution, because it is guided rather than unguided, and it did not necessarily require vast periods of time.

What can we learn about the Fundamentalist impulse from these articles in *The Fundamentals*? First, we learn that the impulse is shared by a wide variety of people. Orr and Warfield were classical Christian scholars. Morgan was pastor of a great church in London. Torrey, among other things, led two Bible institutes and conducted large evangelistic campaigns; later he helped organize the World's Christian Fundamentals Association. Pierson's career was similarly varied and included influential work in Christian missions; he may have coined the famous phrase "the evangelization of the world in this generation." Hague served as an Anglican rector in Canada. Kelly was a surgeon and professor of medicine at Johns Hopkins University.[14, 15] The authors of *The Fundamentals* belonged to different churches in different nations and denominations, and they held views at variance with one another.

On the other hand, we also learn that the writers agreed that biblical criticism, evolution, and liberal theology had secular tendencies that constituted a threat to the faith of the church and that therefore needed to be resisted. These writers were cautious in what they wrote, they paid careful attention to those with whom they disagreed, and they remained courteous toward those whose views they opposed, but they were convinced that biblical criticism, evolution, and liberal theology were so permeated with secular ideas that acceptance of them would lead to secularism and unbelief. For these authors the stakes were high; they were co-belligerents in a struggle for the survival of Christian faith.

Third, we learn that the writers did not present a rounded, balanced summary of the fundamentals of the Christian religion but rather attempted to defend the particular beliefs that happened to be at risk at the time they wrote. This is not in itself a criticism; defending what is at risk is perfectly appropriate. On the other hand, it is important not to ignore the fact that *The Fundamentals* did not contain a balanced summary of the fundamentals of the Christian faith.

To take one obvious example, there is no article on the principal Christian doctrine, which was worked out by the Christian church over the first four centuries of its life and was displayed in the most ecumenical of all creeds, the Nicene Creed. That is the doctrine of the Trinity. *The Fundamentals* contain multiple articles defending, for example, particular understandings of the authorship of various books of the Bible, but they contain no article affirming, explaining, or even defending the doctrine of the Trinity. This imbalance is so extreme that it is not too much to say that one problem with *The Fundamentals* is that they were not fundamental enough. We will return to this point in chapter 6.

Fourth, we learn that the writers defended with equal vigor both universally held Christian beliefs such as Christ's deity and particular beliefs such as the Mosaic authorship of the Pentateuch, the first five books of the Old Testament. Dyson Hague, for example, argued that, since Jesus thought Moses wrote the Pentateuch, to question its authorship by Moses was effectively to deny Jesus' authority. We do not agree with this argument; we do not think Jesus intended to address the question of the authorship of the first books of the Bible, and we think that what is religiously important about those books is their divinely inspired message, not which human being wrote them.

In our judgment, it is misleading to treat a matter like this as if it were a fundamental of the Christian faith. One problem with treating non-fundamental matters as if they are fundamental is that you begin to treat people who disagree about non-fundamental matters as if they disagreed about fundamental ones; you may even begin to assume that such people are not really Christians at all. One of the critics of Fundamentalism, James Barr, has argued that Fundamentalists characteristically want not only to claim the name "Christian" for themselves but also to deny that name to others: "One who wishes to understand fundamentalism must realize that this idea of the true Christian is not accessory but essential . . . . the fundamentalist's position about true and nominal Christianity is intrinsic to his faith: to ask him to modify it is to ask him for something that he cannot perform."[16]

We have spoken of Fundamentalism as one of many expressions of Christian faith, but, of course, that is a description many Fundamentalists would not accept; for them, Fundamentalism is the Christian faith, and non-Fundamentalists who claim to be Christians are in fact pseudo-Christians.

The Five Fundamentals

Our second example of Fundamentalist theology is a list of beliefs variously called "the five fundamentals," "the five points of Fundamentalism," or "the five fundamental beliefs." The complicated story of the five points has been told by Ernest Sandeen and George Marsden.[17] The bottom line is that in 1910 the General Assembly of the Northern Presbyterian Church endorsed five points of doctrine; they were the inerrancy of the original manuscripts of the Bible, the virgin birth of Christ, the substitutionary atonement of Christ, the bodily resurrection of Christ, and the authenticity of the miracles recorded in the Bible. Later on, in the 1920s and afterward, the phrase *five fundamentals* was sometimes used of these five, but sometimes it was used of a slightly altered version that included the deity of Christ, and sometimes it was used of a version in which the premillennial return of Christ was substituted for the authenticity of the miracles.

We will briefly review each of these theological themes, and we will offer comments and evaluations of the Fundamentalists' understanding and use of each one.

Biblical Inerrancy

The first thing to observe about these five themes is that primacy was given to the inerrancy of the Scriptures. Belief in inerrancy became the rallying cry of Fundamentalists, and this has continued into the twenty-first century; Fundamentalists treat biblical inerrancy as the fundamental that supports the other fundamentals.

Although biblical inerrancy has been defined in a variety of ways and continues to be nuanced by its advocates in response to criticisms of the theory,[18] there is widespread agreement that biblical inerrancy means that the original manuscripts of the Bible were free from all error. The original manuscripts are known as *autographs*, that is, *the writings themselves*. Virtually everyone agrees that the autographs were written on scrolls in Hebrew and Greek, were never collected at one place, and were lost centuries ago. Biblical inerrantists believe the autographs were free of errors not only in theology and ethics but also in all other disciplines including history and science.

Since the autographs are no longer extant, why did theologians postulate a theory about them? One reason was that, because they no longer existed, biblical critics could not show that there were errors in them. Another reason was that they thought a perfect God would not have inspired imperfect Scriptures. A third reason was that they thought the Bible's own witness to itself is that it is inerrant. Finally, once inerrancy of the autographs became widely held, many Christians simply came to assume that it was the church's traditional understanding of the Bible.

While there is some truth in these four ideas, there are also problems with all of them. First, the appeal to non-extant manuscripts did not in fact have any effect on biblical criticism; the critics simply proceeded to work with the available manuscripts. Second, if we follow the logic that says a perfect God would not inspire a book with errors, then would we not also have to follow the logic that says a perfect God would not create a church that commits errors? Yet all Protestants reject the Roman Catholic claim that the church cannot commit errors. Third, we certainly agree that the Bible contains numerous references to itself that speak of it as trustworthy and authoritative, but these references are not to non-extant manuscripts but to the copies and translations available at the time; to that extent, at least, these references differ in kind from the claims of biblical inerrantists. Finally, the assumption that the church has always believed in biblical inerrancy seems to us not to be true; we know of no theologians before the nineteenth century who made claims for the autographs that they did not also make for the texts and translations of the Bible which they had in their possession.[19]

Since biblical inerrancy is about non-extant Hebrew and Greek manuscripts only, it is a technical teaching. Concerning the Bible we now have—the modern reconstructions of the Hebrew and Greek texts and the modern translations into languages such as English—sophisticated biblical inerrantists claim neither more nor less than what the church has traditionally claimed, namely, that the Bible is God's inspired Word and the written authority for the faith and life of the church. Sophisticated biblical inerrantists do not claim that the biblical manuscripts we have today are free of errors, though they do tend to avoid the word *error*, preferring to speak instead of *inadvertencies, problems, apparent discrepancies,* or *apparent contradictions* in the Bible.[20]

Since the creation of the doctrine of inerrant autographs in the early nineteenth century, there have been many attempts to refine the doctrine for modern audiences. Probably the most representative and influential product of this work is *The Chicago Statement on Biblical Inerrancy,* created by an interdenominational committee of 268 scholars in 1978.

Ironically, though biblical inerrancy was intended by its supporters to provide for Christians a defense of the truth of the Bible, sometimes it has had the opposite effect—namely, of undermining Christians' confidence in the Bible. By claiming that the Bible cannot err in any matter, inerrantists created a needless dilemma for students of the Bible. For example, the sequence of Jesus' temptations differs in the accounts written by Matthew and Luke; Matthew said Jesus was tempted to throw himself from the Temple before he was tempted to worship Satan, and Luke put it the other way around. Most Christians are completely untroubled by this, as indeed they should be; what matters is that our Lord was tempted and that he successfully resisted the temptations and remained completely obedient to the Father. But an intense interest in precise inerrancy can cause a faithful Christian to wonder if perhaps Matthew or Luke was mistaken and, once that happens, to wonder whether anything else in the Bible is to be trusted.

To us this seems to be an undesirable, though unintended, byproduct of the technical view of inerrancy. Indeed, the issue can become more severe than this. In May 1987, the six seminaries of the Southern Baptist Convention sponsored a Conference on Biblical Inerrancy. At one of the conference workshops, Fisher Humphreys commented that commitment to biblical inerrancy has sometimes "eroded our confidence that the Bible which we now have is itself the very Word of God."[21] In the discussion that followed, one defender of biblical inerrancy said that he had no idea that anyone today believed that the Bible we have today, as opposed to an original manuscript, is literally God's Word. We find this position disturbing, but it is understandable; the price to be paid for focusing too much attention on the non-extant original manuscripts of the Bible is a diminishment of the status of the texts and translations we have today.

Therefore, while we respect those who feel that the best way to affirm the truthfulness of the biblical message is to adopt the technical view of biblical inerrancy, we do not agree with them. For us, the best way to affirm the truthfulness of the biblical message is the way the church has always done it, namely, to affirm that the Bible as we now have it—texts and translations—is the Word of God and the written authority by which the church is to order its life and faith.

There are various ways to express this understanding of biblical authority. We welcome the brief litany used in many churches in which, following the reading of Scripture, the reader says, "This is the Word of God for the people of God," and the people reply, "Thanks be to God." We believe Paul's famous statement about Scripture in 2 Timothy, which contains no reference to original manuscripts or to inerrancy, is a perfectly adequate account of Scripture for the church today. Paul wrote, "All Scripture is given by inspiration of God, and is profitable for doctrine, for reproof, for correction, for instruction in righteousness: That the man of God may be perfect, thoroughly furnished unto all good works."[22]

The Virgin Birth of Christ

The second fundamental belief was the virgin birth of Christ. Ordinary Christians across the centuries have embraced this belief because it is found in the Bible. Belief in the virgin birth gave rise to great devotion for Mary; in the Eastern Orthodox churches she is called *Theotokos*, the bearer of God, and in the Roman Catholic Church she is called *Mother of God.*

Some biblical critics were skeptical about the virgin birth for various reasons. In a book on the Apostles' Creed, the New Testament scholar C. E. B. Cranfield has reviewed six of these reasons.[23]

First, the story of the virgin birth is found only in Matthew and Luke and apparently was unknown to the other writers of the New Testament. Second, the genealogies in Matthew and Luke trace Jesus' ancestry through Joseph rather than through Mary. Third, when Jesus was an adult Mary did not understand him. Fourth, the story of the virgin birth owes its existence to the prophecy found in Isaiah 7:14. Fifth, the story of Jesus' virgin birth came into being in imitation of numerous pagan stories of virgin births. Finally, the virgin birth did not happen because miracles cannot happen.

Cranfield provided impressive arguments against each of these objections, and he concluded by writing, "The arguments urged against the historicity of the virgin birth are by no means as cogent as has often been assumed."[24]

We agree with Cranfield, and, like him, we think Fundamentalists were right that one of the objections to the virgin birth of Christ was a general sense that miracles can't happen, so we shall address this issue below.

The Substitutionary Atonement

The third fundamental was the penal substitutionary atonement of Christ. This is the belief that when Christ died he experienced God's punishment for the sins of human beings. John Calvin carefully worked out this theory of the atonement in the sixteenth century, and since then it has had a large following among both professional theologians and ordinary church members.

In the New Testament there are numerous expressions of the meaning of Jesus' sufferings and death and resurrection: he defeated the devil; he revealed God's love; he paid a price to redeem sinful people; he gave his life as a sacrifice like the sacrifices of the Day of Atonement and those of the Passover; he set an example for his followers who must take up their crosses and follow him; he was the Suffering Servant of Isaiah 53.

An exact count of these understandings of Jesus' work is not possible, but we do know that there are no fewer than twenty of them in the New Testament. Traditionally the church has affirmed all of them; however, at different times in the church's history, one of them has been given more prominence than the others. For example, according to the Swedish theologian Gustaf Aulén, for the first thousand years of its history the church emphasized that by his death Christ had won a victory over the devil.[25]

One reason for the variation in emphasis on understandings of Christ's work is that the Christian church has never affirmed an official doctrine of the atonement, as it did for the Incarnation in the fourth century when it declared Jesus to be one person with two natures. Despite the lack of an official church teaching about the work of Christ, Fundamentalists insisted that true believers must affirm penal substitution.

We said above that Fundamentalists were right when they identified reservations about the virgin birth as originating partially in a reservation about miracles in general. But, so far as we can tell, the reservations about penal substitution did not originate in secularism; many Christians have had reservations about this understanding of Christ's work that have nothing to do with secularism. One concern is that penal substitution is not widely attested in the Scriptures. Some Christians are morally offended by the idea that it was somehow legally necessary for God to punish Christ in order to forgive sinners. Others are troubled about what this theory says about the relationship between the Father and the Son; it suggests that the Father was punishing the Son, whereas Paul had told the

Corinthians that "God was in Christ, reconciling the world unto himself."[26]

When penal substitution became a target of criticism by some liberal theologians, the Fundamentalists lifted up this understanding of Christ's work as a fundamental of the faith. While this was a possible response to the concerns people felt about the theory, it is our judgment that a better response would have been to accept these concerns as legitimate and respond to them accordingly. Several theologians have done this, and we suggest *The Cross of Christ* by John Stott as an excellent example of a book that affirms penal substitution and also provides positive help to people who feel the force of the kind of objections to penal substitution mentioned above.[27] In our judgment, this kind of theological work is a better response to people's reservations than the response of attacking such people as unbelievers.

The Bodily Resurrection of Christ

The fourth fundamental belief was in Christ's bodily resurrection. The key word here is *bodily*. Some liberal theologians of the nineteenth century denied the bodily resurrection of Christ. They pointed to the resurrection stories in the Gospels in support of their denials. In some of these stories, people failed to recognize Jesus. His body was obviously not a normal body since he appeared and vanished mysteriously and passed through walls. Also, it seems impossible to correlate chronologically the various stories of Jesus' appearances after his resurrection. As a result, some liberal Christians came to believe that Jesus' resurrection was spiritual rather than physical; they postulated that the story of an empty tomb was a later addition to the gospel story by well-meaning but misguided disciples.

Fundamentalists felt that this understanding of the resurrection of Christ threatened the supernatural claims of Christianity, and in response they affirmed their belief in the bodily resurrection of Christ as a fundamental tenet of the faith.

In our judgment, the Fundamentalists were right about this. Denying Jesus' bodily resurrection seems to us to undermine a principal part of why the gospel is such good news, and it also seems to us that some of the reservations about the resurrection of Christ, like some of the reservations about the virgin birth, are in fact linked to a general reservation about miracles.

On the other hand, we doubt the wisdom of the manner in which the Fundamentalists dealt with the bodily resurrection of Christ. Though we accept a need for polemics in the church, we believe that a better strategy than the Fundamentalists' would have been to supplement arguments for Jesus' resurrection with a careful unpacking of the meaning of that unique and momentous event. Several contemporary theologians have done this, among them Wolfhart Pannenberg[28] and N. T. Wright.[29] We believe work such as theirs does more to insure the continuance of the church's faith in the risen Lord than do the polemics characteristic of Fundamentalists.

The Historicity of Miracles

The original fifth fundamental was belief in the historicity of the miracles reported in the Bible. This was a wide-ranging belief since it incorporated every purported miracle in the Old and New Testaments, though, as we have seen, Fundamentalists gave special place to the miracles of the virgin birth and bodily resurrection of Christ. Fundamentalists found this affirmation necessary since many scholars had doubts about some or all of the miracle stories in the Bible.

When biblical scholars, acting as historical critics, weigh the evidence for each miracle independently, they find impressive public evidence for some, such as Christ's resurrection, and less impressive public evidence for other miracle stories in the Bible.[30] Because of their view of the Bible, this distinction is not important to Fundamentalists; since they believe the Bible is inerrant and serves as the foundation for their beliefs, it makes no sense to them to believe in the resurrection and not also believe in other miracles.

As we said above, we think the Fundamentalists were right to think that some of the doubts about miracles reported in the Bible arose from secular assumptions. The assumption that miracles can't happen makes sense only if one also assumes either that there is no God at all or that, if there is a God, God cannot act in this world in ways at variance with the orderly processes or laws of nature. Of course, neither of these assumptions is compatible with traditional Christian teaching. It is one thing to question whether a particular story in the Bible is a miracle story; it is another simply to assume God cannot override the regularities by which the world God created operates. It is appropriate to ask whether the author of the story of Jonah and the fish intended to tell a parable or to provide an account of an historical event; that is simply good Bible study. It is not appropriate for Christians to begin their study of the Bible with the assumption that miracles can't happen.

A further issue for Fundamentalism is whether the affirmation of the historicity of miracles recorded in the Bible is a suitable response to secularism. It unmasks secularism, but does it heal it?

The American theologian Reinhold Niebuhr told a story about attending a church service with his wife and hearing her bishop preach a sermon whose first point was that the church "must not be afraid to state that [its message] is both supernatural and miraculous." Niebuhr commented, "I failed to understand just how the bold proclamation of miracles would give modern paganism its *coup de grâce*. . . . Not being a naturalist, I didn't mind his emphasis upon supernaturalism, if he had only said what he meant by it and in what way it was related to the spiritual life."[31] Like Niebuhr, we share Fundamentalism's rejection of secularism and its affirmation of miracles. We also agree with Niebuhr's idea that simply affirming miracles is not enough—we must also offer accounts of what miracles meant to the writers of the Bible and of what they mean to us today.

Premillennialism

In lists of the five fundamental beliefs in the 1920s, the affirmation of premillennialism replaced the affirmation of the historicity of the miracles. We have seen that all of the first Fundamentalists did not believe in premillennialism, but eventually premillennialism became prominent in Fundamentalism. One scholar, Ernest Sandeen, has argued that premillennialism is definitive of Fundamentalism.[32]

Premillennialism is a particular understanding of events at the end of the world. In Revelation 20, and only there, the Bible speaks of a thousand-year reign of Christ upon Earth. Most Christians throughout Christian history have understood this as a symbol; after all, Revelation is filled with symbols. Of those who have believed the millennium is literal, most have been post-millennialists; that is, they have believed the gospel will be so successful throughout the world that most people will welcome Christ when he returns to Earth to reign for a thousand years.

In the nineteenth century, an alternative to these ideas was developed and vigorously promoted at Bible conferences, especially in England and North America. Known as dispensational premillennialism, this was the view that the world will continue to get worse and worse until Christ returns to Earth and takes his people away into heaven; this is called the rapture of the church. On Earth there will be seven years of great tribulation, after which Christ and his people will return to Earth and engage in a great battle called Armageddon, in which Satan and his armies will be defeated. Satan will then be bound, and Christ will reign on Earth for a thousand years. After this the final judgment will take place. Many Christians became convinced that this premillennial teaching was the correct account of the Bible's teaching about the end times.

As we have seen, all of the original Fundamentalists were not premillennialists, but eventually in the movement premillennialism was elevated to the status of a fundamental of the Christian faith.

We think this was a mistake. We know of no way to justify the claim that a particular scenario for the end of the world is a fundamental of the Christian faith. We believe what is fundamental is simply that the future of our world is in God's hands and that God will bring the world to its appropriate end in God's own time and way.

We conclude that, just as war is too important to be left to the generals, so the fundamentals of the Christian faith are too important to be left to Fundamentalists. In the conclusion of this book, we shall offer an alternative account of the fundamentals of the Christian faith, one that we believe is more fundamental than the account of Fundamentalists.

NOTES

[1] James Orr, "The Virgin Birth of Christ," in vol. 1 of *The Fundamentals: A Testimony to the Truth*, 7; reissued in George Marsden, ed., *The Fundamentals* (New York: Garland Publishing, Inc., 1988), I.

[2] Benjamin B. Warfield, "The Deity of Christ," in vol. 1 of *The Fundamentals: A Testimony to the Truth*, 21; reissued in Marsden, ed., *The Fundamentals*, I.

[3] R. A. Torrey, "The Personality and Deity of the Holy Spirit," in vol. 1 of *The Fundamentals: A Testimony to the Truth*, 56; reissued in Marsden, ed., *The Fundamentals*, I.

[4] A. T. Pierson, "The Proof of the Living God," in vol. 1 of *The Fundamentals: A Testimony to the Truth*, 82; reissued in Marsden, ed., *The Fundamentals*, I.

[5] Pierson, "The Proof of the Living God," 85.

[6] Canon Dyson Hague, "History of the Higher Criticism," in vol. 1 of *The Fundamentals: A Testimony to the Truth*, 87-122; reissued in Marsden, ed., *The Fundamentals*, I.

[7] Hague, "History of the Higher Criticism," 91.

[8] Ibid., 92.

[9] Ibid., 110.

[10] Ibid., 115.

[11] Howard A. Kelly, "A Personal Testimony," in vol. 1 of *The Fundamentals: A Testimony to the Truth*, 123; reissued in Marsden, ed., *The Fundamentals*, I.

[12] James Orr, "Science and Christian Faith," in vol. 1 of *The Fundamentals: A Testimony to the Truth*, 123; reissued in Marsden, ed., *The Fundamentals*, vol. 4, pp. 95-96.

[13] Orr, "Science and Christian Faith," 103.

[14] Biographical information about Torrey, Pierson, and Hague is taken from articles about them in Daniel G. Reid, coordinating ed., *Dictionary of Christianity in America* (Downers Grove IL: InterVarsity Press, 1990).

[15] We find it interesting that Kelly was a friend of the agnostic newspaperman H. L. Mencken, and Mencken has provided an account of Kelly's witnessing to him while they rode together on a train from Washington to their homes in Baltimore. See Joel A. Carpenter, *Revive Us Again: The Reawakening of American Fundamentalism* (New York: Oxford University Press, 1997), 79.

[16] James Barr, *Fundamentalism* (Philadelphia: The Westminster Press, 1978), 17.

[17] Ernest R. Sandeen, *The Roots of Fundamentalism: British and American Millenarianism, 1800–1930* (Chicago: The University of Chicago Press, 1970), xiv-xv, 251-53; George Marsden, *Fundamentalism and American Culture: The Shaping of Twentieth-century Evangelicalism, 1870–1925* (Oxford: Oxford University Press, 1980), 262, n. 30.

[18] David S. Dockery, "Variations on Inerrancy," *SBC Today* (May 1986): 10-11.

[19] Jack Rogers, "The Church Doctrine of Biblical Authority," in *Biblical Authority*, ed. Jack Rogers (Waco: Word Books, 1977).

[20] See, for example, L. Russ Bush and Tom J. Nettles, *Baptists and the Bible* (Chicago: Moody Press, 1980), 414.

[21] Fisher Humphreys, "The Baptist Faith and Message and the Chicago Statement on Biblical Inerrancy," in *The Proceedings of the Conference on Biblical Inerrancy 1987* (Nashville: Broadman Press, 1987), 329.

[22] 2 Timothy 3:16-17 (King James Version).

[23] C. E. B. Cranfield, *The Apostles' Creed* (Grand Rapids: William B. Eerdmans Publishing Company, 1993), ch. 6.

[24] Cranfield, *The Apostles' Creed*, 29.

[25] Gustaf Aulén, *Christus Victor*, trans. A. G. Hebert (London: SPCK, 1965).

[26] 2 Corinthians 5:19 (KJV).

[27] John R. W. Stott, *The Cross of Christ* (Downers Grove IL: InterVarsity Press, 1986).

[28] Wolfhart Pannenberg, *Jesus—God and Man*, trans. Lewis L. Wilkins and Duane A. Priebe (Philadelphia: The Westminster Press, 1968), ch. 3.

[29] Wright has written and spoken about Christ's resurrection in many venues. For an especially readable example, see Tom Wright, *The Original Jesus* (Grand Rapids: William B. Eerdmans Publishing Company, 1996), ch. 6. For a closely reasoned case addressed to his

fellow academics, see N. T. Wright, *The Resurrection of the Son of God* (Minneapolis: Fortress Press, 2003), especially chs. 18-19.

[30] We find compelling the essay on the nature of the evidence for Christ's resurrection titled "The Events of Easter and the Empty Tomb" by the Roman Catholic church historian Hans von Campenhausen; see his *Tradition and Life in the Church*, trans. A. V. Littledale (Philadelphia: Fortress Press, 1960), ch. 3.

[31] Reinhold Niebuhr, *Essays in Applied Christianity* (New York: Meridian Books, 1960), 45.

[32] Ernest R. Sandeen, *The Roots of Fundamentalism.*

CHAPTER 4

THE ATTITUDES OF FUNDAMENTALISM

Although *fundamentalism* is primarily a theological designation, it is also a term that refers to a set of attitudes. One historian of Fundamentalism, C. Allyn Russell, has observed, "More typical and distinguishing . . . than any of the doctrines that fundamentalists embraced was their characteristic attitude."[1]

Many of the attitudes that came to be associated with the original American Fundamentalism are common to various forms of fundamentalism. This commonality is one of the reasons the term *fundamentalist* can meaningfully be used to describe people in various faiths.

Attitudes common to the various forms of fundamentalism include suspicion, fear, anger, and separatism. While other attitudes might be included in this list, these seem to us to be representative.

Suspicion

Suspicion is feeling that something or someone is wrong without proof or on slight evidence. Most people are suspicious at some point in their lives. For many Fundamentalists, though, suspicion is a continuing state of mind. Because Fundamentalism is predicated on the theory that liberals are trying to subvert the church, Fundamentalists are especially suspicious of liberals. Many of them constantly check the theology of others to insure that they are not liberals. This causes Fundamentalists to be suspicious of those inside their community as well as those outside it.

This suspicion can and often does escalate to a kind of paranoia. Fundamentalists tend to subscribe to the domino theory: if you surrender one idea, eventually you will surrender all the others as well. If people hold a liberal position on one issue, then they are suspected of holding other liberal views. This causes Fundamentalists to feel that they must be constantly diligent in assessing the beliefs of others.

Fear

Fear is a common human emotion, and it is appropriate to feel fear about many things in life.

Fundamentalism was born from the fear that aspects of the modern world were threatening the faith of the Christian community, and many Fundamentalists continue to live their lives in an elevated state of fear. Their fear is predicated on the idea that the world is evil and that true believers must be constantly vigilant in order to avoid secularism.

This fear is heightened by exposure to higher education. One of the reasons many Fundamentalists became anti-intellectuals was their fear of the influence of intellectuals. It is not uncommon for Fundamentalist students to be urged not to allow themselves to be changed by their education in secular, or even in religious, colleges and universities.

Anger

Anger is another common human emotion. People feel anger in response to a variety of experiences, and Fundamentalists are not alone in having anger.

But in Fundamentalism, anger seems to be understood as an appropriate motivator, and so it is cultivated. "A fundamentalist is an evangelical who is mad about something," Jerry Falwell has written. Even though he said these words tongue in cheek, they are effective communication because there is a grain of truth in them.[2]

Part of Fundamentalist anger can be traced to the fear Fundamentalists experience. Their perception that liberalism constitutes a threat to their values and beliefs creates an environment in which they feel they must fight to survive. George Marsden defined Fundamentalism as "a loose, diverse, and changing federation of co-belligerents united by their fierce opposition to modernist attempts to bring Christianity in line with modern thought."[3] That belligerence is easily observable. It is not uncommon for someone who hears Fundamentalist preaching for the first time to ask, "Why is the preacher so angry?" The novelist Anne Lamott has offered a wise principle that applies to all Christians, including Fundamentalists: "You can safely assume that you've created God in your own image when it turns out that God hates all the same people you do."[4]

Separatism

Since Fundamentalists perceive liberals to be a threat to Christianity, they must distance themselves from liberals. This separatism causes Fundamentalists to label others as being "with us" or "against us."

Even those within the Fundamentalist family must be watched, since they may choose the wrong path or weaken in the faith at any time. To accept those who have aberrant views on any of the fundamentals, and often on lesser subjects, is to condone heresy. This explains the frequent splits that occur in Fundamentalist churches and the need to purge liberals or compromisers from Fundamentalist groups.

In Fundamentalism there is a tradition of second-degree separatism. This is separation from people who are Fundamentalists themselves but who are willing to relate to and work with people who are not Fundamentalists. In some Fundamentalist circles there is contempt for conservative Christians who are irenic. Bob Jones III has described such people as *pseudo-Fundamentalists*.[5] George W. Dollar, a historian of Fundamentalism who is a Fundamentalist, has described how in 1978 Fundamentalist Wendell Mullen condemned John R. Rice because Rice had supported Jerry Falwell, who had sinned by standing next to Warren Wiersbe, who had approvingly quoted Helmut Thielicke, who was not an inerrantist.[6]

These four attitudes—suspicion, fear, anger, and separatism—are closely linked to each other, and one way to deal with them is to deal with them as a group. This seems to have been recognized by Ed Dobson and Ed Hindson, two Fundamentalist leaders who have acknowledged the following about themselves and their fellow Fundamentalists:

> Because of its strong commitment to biblical truth, Fundamentalism tends to level scathing criticisms at Liberalism and the ecumenical movement, and, in general all ecclesiastical groups and organizations that are not a part of its own movement. . . . Fundamentalism must avoid the extreme tendency to blast, label, and excommunicate anyone and everyone who raises even the slightest objection to its beliefs and methods.[7]

Alternative Attitudes

Attitudes are important in any religious movement. A. W. Tozer, who died in 1963, was an editor and pastor in Chicago during the middle part of the twentieth century. He was a leading inspirational writer among Fundamentalists. Many of his writings are still in print and are widely read in Fundamentalist circles. Nevertheless, he recognized the attitudinal shortcomings of Fundamentalism. In a book titled *The Pursuit of Man: The Divine Conquest of the Human Heart*, he wrote,

> The blight of the Pharisee's heart in olden times was doctrine without love. With the teachings of the Pharisees Christ had little quarrel, but with the pharisaic spirit He carried on unceasing warfare to the end. It was religion that put Christ on the cross, religion without the indwelling Spirit. It is no use to deny that Christ was crucified by persons who would today be called fundamentalists.[8]

E. J. Carnell, an evangelical critic of Fundamentalism, said "the mark of a true disciple is *love*, not doctrine."[9]

There are alternatives to suspicion, fear, anger, and separatism, and we believe they are more appropriate than these attitudes. Instead of suspicion, we ought to trust people until we know we can't. They don't have to prove themselves—they have to disprove themselves. We have learned from New Testament scholar Malcolm Tolbert that Christ taught and modeled trust in others. "We should," Tolbert said, "always think the best about others." Suspicion makes that impossible.

Suspicion can generate fear. Fear is one attitude that is never seen in Christ. Even in the face of death, he was unafraid. One of the things Christ does for us is to free us from our fears: "Perfect love casts out fear."[10] A life of fear for the faithful is a contradiction. Instead of fear, Christians should trust God that, in the end, everything is going to be all right. When the English theologian Benedicta Ward was asked what advice she would offer to American evangelical Christians, she replied, "Love and do not be afraid."[11]

Unlike fear, anger is an emotion Jesus did experience. When Philip Wise was a boy, he was told that Jesus never got *angry*. Instead, he was told, Jesus had *righteous indignation*; to suggest that Jesus ever got angry was close to accusing Jesus of sin. A close reading of the New Testament makes the subtle distinction between anger and righteous indignation unconvincing. Jesus did become angry. However, his anger wasn't directed at liberals; it was directed at people who were legalistic, self-righteous, and hypocritical.

Separatism is the rejection of others. This is always harmful for the church. Christians are urged in the New Testament to accept fellow believers. This means affirming as fellow Christians everyone who confesses faith in the crucified and risen Jesus. You do this even if that person makes what you believe to be a serious theological or moral error. You respond to such errors, if it is appropriate for you to do so at all, at an appropriate time and by means of friendly discussion, not with anger or by separation. This is the model for church discipline.

Conclusion

Often the greatest harm done by Fundamentalism is not theological but personal. The reason the term *fundamentalism* has become pejorative is that fundamentalism has hurt so many people deeply.

In a 2003 interview in *Baptists Today*, former President Jimmy Carter was asked to comment on his Nobel Lecture in which he said, "The present era is a challenging and disturbing time for those whose lives are shaped by religious faith based on kindness towards each other." Carter said:

> There is a remarkable trend, in my opinion, toward fundamentalism in all the religions—including the different denominations of Christianity as well as Hinduism, Judaism, and Islam.
>
> Increasingly, it seems to me, people are inclined to align themselves uniquely with God and then to begin a process of deciding: "Since I am aligned with God, I am superior and my beliefs should prevail. And anyone who disagrees with me is inherently wrong."
>
> Then the next step is inherently inferior, and the ultimate step is subhuman, and then their lives are not significant.
>
> So that tendency has created—throughout the world, in fact—intense religious conflicts. It is generally characterized by the word fundamentalism.
>
> "I am right; and everyone who disagrees with me is inherently wrong and inferior. If you want to participate in my organization or life, you must comply completely with what I ordain as proper religious faith. . . ."
>
> Those who resist the inclination toward fundamentalism—to continue the same basic premise—and who truly follow the nature, actions, and words of Jesus Christ—who in my opinion ordained to us through his own teachings that we should expand our lives and not be exclusionary, but that we should encompass—with our care and generosity and forgiveness and compassion and unselfish love—people who are remarkably different from us. . . .
>
> It is not easy to do. It is a natural human inclination to encapsulate ourselves in a superior fashion with people who are just like us—and to assume that we are fulfilling

the mandate of our lives if we can just confine our love to our own family or people who are just like us. But that breaking through the barrier and reaching out to others is what personifies a Christian and what emulates the role that Christ set as a perfect example for us.[12]

We believe President Carter is right. Those of us committed to following Jesus Christ need to trust people rather than be suspicious of them. We need to love rather than be afraid. We need to feel sorrow for rather than anger at victims of secularism. And we need to unite with fellow Christians rather than separate from them.

NOTES

[1] C. Allyn Russell, *Voices of American Fundamentalism: Seven Biographical Studies* (Philadelphia: The Westminster Press, 1976), 10.

[2] Jerry Falwell, *Falwell: An Autobiography* (Lynchburg: Liberty House Publishers, 1997), 385.

[3] George Marsden, *Fundamentalism and American Culture: The Shaping of Twentieth-century Evangelicalism, 1870–1925* (Oxford: Oxford University Press, 1980), 4.

[4] Anne Lamott, *Bird by Bird: Some Instructions on Writing and Life* (New York: Anchor Books, 1994), 22. We thank Mike Hardin for locating this quotation.

[5] Bob Jones III, "Pseudo-Fundamentalists: The New Breed in Sheep's Clothing." This statement is available online at <http://www.bju.edu/resources/faith/1978/issue1/pseudo.html>.

[6] George W. Dollar, *The Fight for Fundamentalism: American Fundamentalism, 1973–1983* (Sarasota FL: self-published, 1983), 113.

[7] Ed Dobson and Ed Hindson, *The Fundamentalist Phenomenon: The Resurgence of Conservative Christianity* (Garden City: Doubleday & Company, Inc., 1981), 179.

[8] A. W. Tozer, *The Pursuit of Man: The Divine Conquest of the Human Heart* (Camp Hill: Christian Publications, 1997), 106.

[9] Edward John Carnell, *The Case for Orthodox Theology* (Philadelphia: The Westminster Press, 1959), 128.

[10] 1 John 4:18.

[11] Michael Bauman, *Roundtable: Conversations with European Theologians* (Grand Rapids: Baker Book House, 1990), 106.

[12] *Baptists Today* (November 2003): 16.

CHAPTER 5

FUNDAMENTALISM AND SOUTHERN BAPTISTS

In this chapter we address some of the special concerns of Southern Baptists and former Southern Baptists who are not Fundamentalists; we shall refer to this audience as *progressive Baptists*. Progressive Baptists who are interested in Fundamentalism need a general account of relationships between Fundamentalism and Southern Baptists, and in this chapter we offer a brief such account.

We begin with general observations. In the early twentieth century, Southern Baptists did not experience in their denominational life as much of the influence of liberalism as did other denominations in the United States. As a result, most Southern Baptists did not become especially alarmed about liberalism. When efforts were made to recruit Southern Baptists into the Fundamentalist movement, most resisted. They felt that their traditional Baptist beliefs and practices were better alternatives to secularism than Fundamentalism. One result of this was that some Fundamentalist leaders criticized Southern Baptists as having compromised with liberalism.

Despite their general aloofness from the Fundamentalist movement, Southern Baptists were not impervious to Fundamentalist influences, and many Southern Baptists became familiar with particular Fundamentalist ideas and embraced them. Some also embraced Fundamentalist attitudes, which is understandable given that suspicion, fear, anger, and separation come naturally to human beings. Those who did this did not always realize they were departing from Baptist traditions, and, in time, some of them came to assume that the Baptist tradition was in fact a Fundamentalist tradition.

We have selected two stories from Southern Baptist history in the twentieth century to illustrate these general statements, one from the first half of the century and the other from the second half. They are the story of J. Frank Norris and the story of the new directions taken by the Southern Baptist Convention following the controversy that began in 1979.

J. Frank Norris[1]

J. Frank Norris was born in Alabama in 1877 and was converted in a brush arbor revival meeting at age thirteen. He attended Baylor University in Waco, Texas, and the Southern Baptist Theological Seminary in Louisville, Kentucky. In 1909 he became pastor of the First Baptist Church of Fort Worth, a position he held until his death forty-three years later. Norris was one of the first pastors in the nation to make use of radio. In 1927 he renamed a newspaper he controlled *The Fundamentalist.* In 1931 he founded a Bible institute. In 1935 he became pastor of the Temple Baptist Church in Detroit while continuing to serve as pastor of the Fort Worth church; he commuted between the two cities by train and plane. He held evangelistic crusades in various cities, and thousands of converts were added to the churches. He died while on a preaching assignment in Florida in 1952.

Even Norris's enemies acknowledged that he was a powerful preacher and leader, and even his admirers admitted that he was a combative and violent man. Early in his pastorate he was charged with burning down his church's building, but he was acquitted. In 1926 in his office in Fort Worth, he shot and killed D. E. Chipps, a friend of the Roman Catholic Mayor of Fort Worth, H. C. Meacham; Norris was indicted for murder, but at trial a jury found him not guilty.

Norris was combative in his relationships with other ministers and churches. In 1914 he led his church to oppose a program of missions sponsored by Texas Baptists. In 1919 he did the same thing with a program called the 75 Million Campaign sponsored by the Southern Baptist Convention. In 1921 he began a series of attacks against Baylor University because, he said, evolution and infidelity were being taught there. He also attacked individuals. According to Texas legend, he gave J. W. Dawson, pastor of the First Baptist Church of Waco, a free, lifetime subscription to *The Fundamentalist*. In 1940 he sent a letter to George W. Truett, pastor of the First Baptist Church of Dallas, reminding him that Norris's work was prospering; he sent the letter by special delivery so that it would arrive on a Sunday morning just before Truett entered the pulpit, though an associate of Truett intercepted it.[2]

One gets some sense of Norris's style of verbal combat in the following excerpt from one of his sermons:

> These preachers who masquerade under the livery of heaven—I don't care how many degrees they have after their names—LLd's, DD's—Asses, they are infidels when they deny the word of God. . . . I have more respect for

> Tom Paine in his grave, and Bob Ingersoll—at least they
> had self-respect enough to stay out of the church and out
> of the pulpits—they were not like these little modernistic,
> lick-the-skillet, two-by-four aping, asinine preachers, who
> want to be in the priest's office . . . . Oh! some sister will
> say, "I don't think that's the Christian spirit,"—Honey,
> you wouldn't know the Christian spirit, any more than a
> bull would know Shakespeare.[3]

So combative was Norris that it was only a matter of time until he
came into conflict with his fellow Fundamentalists. Here is how one
historian has described that:

> Some fundamentalist leaders seemed destined to become
> separatists by virtue of their personalities. J. Frank
> Norris, for instance, was a violent person who relished
> agitation and conflict, and he felt driven to build his own
> empire. His thirty years' war against the Southern Baptist
> officials was characterized by a steady stream of character
> assaults and political maneuverings. By the end of his
> career, Norris had alienated not only the Convention
> loyalists but militant allies such as Robert T. Ketcham,
> John R. Rice, William Bell Riley, and even his former
> associate pastor, G. Beauchamp Vick.[4]

Given Norris's combativeness, it is understandable that in 1922
the association of Southern Baptist churches in Fort Worth expelled
Norris's church from its membership and that the Baptist General
Convention of Texas permanently excluded him in 1924. In the
following years Norris continued his attacks on fellow ministers and
churches. According to Barry Hankins, "Holding tent meetings
adjacent to the Southern Baptist Convention's annual meeting for
the purpose of disrupting the denomination was one of Norris's
favorite maneuvers."[5]

Unable to draw the Fort Worth association, the Texas state convention, or the Southern Baptist Convention into the Fundamentalist movement, Norris became one of the principal leaders of several organizations not affiliated with his denomination, including the World's Christian Fundamentals Association (1919), the Baptist Bible Union of America (1923), and the Pre-Millennial Baptist Missionary Fellowship (1933).

What may be learned from the story of this extraordinary Fundamentalist leader? We believe the primary lesson is that Southern Baptist leaders, people, and institutions rejected the leadership of J. Frank Norris. Though some individuals and some churches in Southern Baptist circles were willing to follow Norris, a large majority rejected his version of Fundamentalism.

This is not to say that the majority of Southern Baptists were liberals; they were not. It is rather that the majority did not accept Norris's characterization of Southern Baptist institutions as liberal, and furthermore that they felt the better alternative to liberalism was their traditional Baptist theology rather than Fundamentalism.

Even so, to repeat what we said in the introduction to this chapter, as they resisted Norris's offer of Fundamentalism, many individual Southern Baptists were also being influenced by individual themes of Fundamentalist theology. Ideas that originated outside Baptist circles entered into the lives of many Southern Baptists. For example, there has never been a major Baptist confession of faith that affirms premillennialism, but during the twentieth century many Southern Baptists came to embrace that view.

In the end, though, Southern Baptists in the 1920s rejected Norris's offer of Fundamentalism, and we believe that is the principal point of his story.

The New Directions in the Southern Baptist Convention

Beginning in 1979, the Southern Baptist Convention experienced a prolonged, disruptive controversy, two outcomes of which were that all of the agencies of the Convention now have new leaders and the general direction of the Convention has been altered.[6]

Those opposed to the new directions in the Convention routinely say the Convention has become a Fundamentalist organization. As we said earlier in this book, the word *Fundamentalist* has become pejorative, and we think that frequently this word is being used of the Convention in order to discredit the directions taken in the Convention. We do not intend to do that.

Nevertheless, when we have fully discounted this rhetorical use of the word *Fundamentalist* of the new directions in the Convention, four questions emerge. First, are there any identifiable connections between the original Fundamentalist movement and the present Southern Baptist Convention? Second, do the new directions in the Southern Baptist Convention, as a matter of fact, display the family resemblances of fundamentalism we described in chapter 1? Third, do the new leaders in the Convention in general share the theology associated with the original Fundamentalism described in chapter 3? Finally, do the new directions taken by the Convention display the attitudes that have come to be associated with Fundamentalism?

These seem to us to be fair questions, and the answer seems to us in each case to be yes.

Personal Connections

First, there are connections between the original Fundamentalist movement and the Southern Baptist Convention. For example, J. Frank Norris's church, the First Baptist Church of Fort Worth, has re-entered Southern Baptist life. Also, the church of Jerry Falwell, Thomas Road Baptist Church in Lynchburg, Virginia, is now participating in the life of the Southern Baptist Convention; earlier it had participated only in the Baptist Bible Fellowship, an independent Fundamentalist group. There are other examples of bridges being built between heirs of the original Fundamentalist movement and the new Southern Baptist Convention.

We do not in principle object to building bridges to separated Christians. We are committed ecumenists, and we believe it is a good thing to build bridges to all kinds of Christians. The point we make here is that the return of Fundamentalist churches to the Convention says something about the new directions in the Convention, namely, that they are favorable to Fundamentalist churches and Christians.

Generic Characteristics of Fundamentalism

The new directions in the Convention share the family resemblances denominated by the word *fundamentalist*. In chapter 1 we described nine of these resemblances, and we will show now why we think each of them is apparent in the new directions of the Convention.

Fundamentalism has its origins in religion. That is true of the new directions in the Convention. During the heat of the controversy that began in 1979, some who opposed the new leaders said the real issues were not theological but political. In our judgment, this was a false alternative; the real issues were both theological and political. The new leaders of the Convention believed, and still believe today, that the Convention was losing its religious and theological balance.

Second, fundamentalists make selective use of their tradition. The new leaders of the Convention have appealed to some beliefs in the Baptist tradition, but they also have rejected other beliefs in that tradition. An example of a Baptist tradition that has been rejected by the new leaders is congregational decision-making, the idea that the best way for a congregation to discover the mind of Christ is for every member to have an equal voice in decision-making. The new leaders in the Convention do not agree with this Baptist belief; they believe the pastor has more authority than other members. One of the new leaders has written, "An authoritative ministry must be persuasive to fulfill its scriptural mandate. Conversely, a merely persuasive ministry will not suffice."[7]

The new leaders have also expressed reservations about the separation of church and state, a conviction securely rooted in the Baptist tradition. For example, in 1991 the Southern Baptist Convention adopted a resolution approving of "choice in education initiatives which include proper tax incentives for families." For decades the Convention had opposed government support for parochial schools, but, under the new leaders, in 1991 it reversed itself and began to welcome that support. In our judgment, this is the greatest theological tragedy in the history of the Southern Baptist Convention. It seems to us probable that the Convention's retreat from the traditional Baptist conviction about the separation of church and state has contributed to the dramatic shift in American public policy concerning private schools. Recently the problem has been compounded by a ruling of the Supreme Court that declared government vouchers for children who attend private schools as constitutional. In any case, the point is that the new directions in the Convention cannot be described as a comprehensive retrieval of Baptist tradition, but as a selective retrieval.

Third, fundamentalism is a reaction to aspects of the modern world. Of course, all Christians react to aspects of the modern world; all oppose, for example, the worldwide dissemination of child pornography.

The problem is that the new directions in the Convention are opposed to aspects of the modern world that seem good to many people. For example, in 1998 the Convention called upon wives to be submissive to their husbands without also calling upon husbands to be submissive to their wives. Also, in 2000 the Convention officially adopted the view that women may not serve as pastors of churches. Consistent with this, the Convention has decided to discontinue its long-time practice of endorsing women to serve as chaplains in the military.

Fourth, fundamentalists feel their faith is threatened by the modern world. From the beginning of the controversy, the new leaders argued that the theological directions the Convention was then taking constituted a threat to the Convention's faith and life. Here is how one of them expressed it: "The threats to evangelism and missions posed by classical liberalism and neoorthodoxy are well known. For many conservatives, the controversy in Southern Baptist life is a battle for the souls of men."[8]

Fifth, fundamentalists are militant in opposing the aspects of modern life that they find threatening. The controversy in the Southern Baptist Convention was a militant and successful campaign against directions in the Convention's life prior to 1979.

Sixth, authoritarian male leaders lead fundamentalist movements. The principal leaders of the new Southern Baptist Convention are males, and, as noted earlier, in 2000 the Convention revised its confession of faith so that it now says only males may serve as pastors of churches.

Seventh, fundamentalists have a particular view of history. They see the past as better than the present; they see the present as a time of crisis; and they see the future as a time when their cause will be victorious. All of this is true of the new leaders of the Convention. They have repeatedly appealed to a past in which, they believe, virtually all Southern Baptists embraced their ideas. During the controversy, they described the current time as a crisis in which the future of the Convention would be determined, either for good or for ill. And they looked forward to a future in which their ideas would be dominant in the Convention, which is now the case.

Eighth, fundamentalists set definite boundaries and are prepared to take steps that scandalize outsiders if taking these steps will clarify who is an insider and who is an outsider. The new leaders of the Convention have done this. They have redrawn the circle of which views are acceptable and which are not, and they have taken extreme steps to make the boundaries clear. Perhaps the most extreme step taken by the Convention concerns seventy-seven missionaries who served under the International Mission Board of the Southern Baptist Convention.

In 2000, the Southern Baptist Convention adopted a revised version of its confessional statement, which is called "The Baptist Faith and Message." The revision added to the earlier versions this new sentence: "While both men and women are gifted for service in the church, the office of pastor is limited to men as qualified by Scripture."[9] While this had doubtless been the view of the majority of Southern Baptists, it had not been the unanimous view, and for many years some men and women who believed that women may serve as pastors had served as missionaries of the Convention. When the International Mission Board required all its missionaries to accept the new confessional statement, seventy-seven refused to do so; some of them were forced to retire or resign, and those who refused to do either were fired.

Some of the missionaries gave a second reason for their refusal to assent to the revised statement. In the earlier confession, the article on Scripture had the following final sentence: "The criterion by which the Bible is to be interpreted is Jesus Christ." That sentence was removed from the revised version in 2000 to the dismay of many people, including many missionaries. The new leaders defended this action by saying they removed the sentence because it had been called upon to support the view that accepts the authority of Jesus' statements in the New Testament but not the authority of the remainder of the New Testament. Unconvinced by this explanation, many progressive Baptists objected to the omission of what seemed to them to be one of the wisest sentences in "The Baptist Faith and Message."

It is difficult to think of a more extreme step for a Christian denomination to take than to dismiss dozens of faithful missionaries for refusal to conform to a new and innovative concept, which has been added to a document that is supposed to be a confession of faith rather than a creed.

Nor has the process ended. In fall 2003, a professor of missions at the Southeastern Baptist Theological Seminary, Dr. Keith Eitel, wrote an open letter criticizing the International Mission Board for working with other "Great Commission Christians" on the mission field. According to stories by the Associated Baptist Press, Eitel charged that these partnerships have "no mechanisms in place to filter or check the entry of unbiblical practices other than the specific theological preparation of the individual missionary." He accused mission coordinators of "frequently leading their teams to partner with theologically suspect organizations." Ironically, many of the organizations with whom the Southern Baptist missionaries now work cooperatively are Fundamentalist groups who until recently had refused to work with Southern Baptists because they considered Southern Baptists to be suspect.

Friends of ours have expressed surprise that this professor made such a statement, but there is no reason to be surprised. This is simply one more step in the same direction the new leaders of the Convention have been traveling since 1979, and there is no reason to suppose there will not be other steps in this direction. Abstractly stated, there is no logical end to this process; once an organization is committed to careful policing of clear boundaries, willing to take extreme steps to distinguish insiders and outsiders, and determined to keep the outsiders outside, there is nothing to prevent the process from continuing indefinitely. Logically, it does not ever need to stop. It only stops when people decide to stop it.

Ninth and finally, fundamentalists do not work toward cooperation with their opponents but rather attempt to control their community and to implement their program in its entirety. That is the case with the new leaders of the Convention. During the controversy, some of the new leaders spoke about the need for parity on the faculties of the six Southern Baptist seminaries; this was understood to mean they wanted the seminaries to employ some faculty members who agreed with the views of the new leaders. But since the new leaders have attained positions of leadership in the Convention, there has been no more talk about parity; today all faculty at these seminaries share the views of the new leaders.

Themes of Fundamentalist Theology

The new leaders of the Southern Baptist Convention generally share the principal themes of Fundamentalist theology.

We have seen that one of those themes is the inerrancy of the original manuscripts of the Bible in all matters, including history and science as well as faith and morals. Throughout the controversy in the Southern Baptist Convention, the people who lead the Convention today affirmed repeatedly that no issue was more important to them than biblical inerrancy. One of them has expressed vividly a principle that compelled him to work tirelessly and sacrificially for more than twenty years: "Standing upon the complete trustworthiness of God's Word was a hill on which to die."[10] A thoughtful presentation of the inerrancy of the Bible was recommended as the annual doctrinal study book in the churches in 1992.[11]

The original Fundamentalists affirmed, against all naturalistic accounts, the reality of biblical miracles and emphasized the miracles of the virgin birth and bodily resurrection of Christ. The new leaders of the Convention share the concern about naturalistic accounts of the biblical miracles, and they have emphasized the historical reality of the miracles recorded in the Bible.

The original Fundamentalists believed in the substitutionary atonement of Christ, and that is the view of the new leaders in the Convention; they added the word "substitutionary" to the 2000 "Baptist Faith and Message."

The original Fundamentalists affirmed the premillennial understanding of events at the end of the world, and that also has been affirmed by the new leaders. One of the new leaders linked biblical inerrancy, substitutionary atonement, and premillennial eschatology in a memorable phrase, "The Bible, the blood, and the blessed hope."[12]

We have seen that the original Fundamentalists affirmed their theology as a reaction to liberalism, which they understood to be the thin edge of the wedge of secularism. Throughout the controversy, the new leaders affirmed that they were opposing liberal theology because they saw it leading to unbelief; they were in "a battle for the souls of men."[13]

The Attitudes of Fundamentalism

The attitudes of suspicion, fear, anger, and separatism are closely tied to each other, and all of them have been at work in the Convention. We see this in the determination of the new leaders of the Convention to disengage from those who do not share their vision, a determination evident in the decision of the Executive Committee in 2004 to recommend that the Southern Baptist Convention sever all its ties with the Baptist World Alliance. The Alliance is ninety-nine years old; Southern Baptists were among its principal founders and, until recently, they also were among its most enthusiastic supporters. The Executive Committee has cited several reasons for its recommendation, the burden of which is that the Convention should not be working with people with whom they disagree.[14]

Conclusion

Though relationships between Fundamentalism and the Southern Baptist Convention have been complex, it is possible to make general statements that give an accurate overview of the history of these relationships. We will offer five such statements.

First, Southern Baptists rejected the original Fundamentalism, even when it was offered by one of the most effective of all Fundamentalist leaders, J. Frank Norris.

Second, since 1979 the Southern Baptist Convention has re-admitted churches and individuals who are lineal descendants of the original Fundamentalism.

Third, the Convention has moved in new directions that display the family resemblances shared by fundamentalist movements in the various religions.

Fourth, the new leaders of the Convention share the theology associated with the original Fundamentalism. They share Fundamentalism's interpretation of liberalism as a secularizing ideology and they share Fundamentalism's conviction that its theology is the best antidote to liberalism.

Finally, the four attitudes associated with Fundamentalism are at work in the Convention.

In view of this, we believe it is not necessarily unkind or contemptuous to describe the directions of the Convention today as *Fundamentalist*; we think one way to understand those directions is to recognize their family resemblances to generic fundamentalism and to the original Fundamentalism.

NOTES

[1] Of numerous accounts of the life and work of J. Frank Norris, we have drawn especially upon the readable survey found in chapter 2 of *Voices of American Fundamentalism* by C. Allyn Russell (Philadelphia: The Westminster Press, 1976); upon a sympathetic vignette in *The Fundamentalist Phenomenon: The Resurgence of Conservative Christianity* by Ed Dobson and Ed Hindson (Garden City: Doubleday & Company, Inc., 1981), 92-95; upon a critical study by Barry Hankins, *God's Rascal: J. Frank Norris & the Beginnings of Southern Fundamentalism* (Lexington: The University Press of Kentucky, 1996); upon the lively and shrewd interpretation in Walter B. Shurden, *Not a Silent People* (Macon: Smyth & Helwys Publishing, Inc., 1995); and upon the splendid history by Joel A. Carpenter titled *Revive Us Again: The Reawakening of American Fundamentalism* (New York: Oxford University Press, 1997).

[2] Hankins, *God's Rascal,* 133.

[3] Dobson and Hindson, *The Fundamentalist Phenomenon,* 93. Thomas Paine (1736–1809) and Robert Ingersoll (1833–1899) were famous atheists.

[4] Carpenter, *Revive Us Again,* 51.

[5] Hankins, *God's Rascal,* 183, n. 36.

[6] The literature on the controversy and its effects is vast and growing. Out of many fine books, we mention only five: Nancy Tatom Ammerman, *Baptist Battles* (New Brunswick: Rutgers University Press, 1990); Grady C. Cothen, *What Happened to the Southern Baptist Convention?* (Macon: Smyth & Helwys Publishing, 1993); Bill J. Leonard, *God's Last and Only Hope* (Grand Rapids: William B. Eerdmans Publishing Company, 1990); David T. Morgan, *The New Crusades, The New Holy Land* (Tuscaloosa: The University of Alabama Press, 1996); and Walter B. Shurden, ed., *The Struggle for the Soul of the SBC* (Macon: Mercer University Press, 1993). Jerry Sutton provided an authoritative interpretation of the controversy from the point of view of the new leaders of the Convention in *The Baptist Reformation* (Nashville: Broadman & Holman Publishers, 2000).

[7] Richard Land, "Pastoral Leadership: Authoritarian or Persuasive?" in *The Theological Educator* 33 (Spring 1988): 75.

[8] Paige Patterson, "Stalemate," *The Theological Educator* 30 (1985): 2.

[9] "Baptist Faith and Message," article 6. See <http://www.sbc.net/bfm/bfm2000.asp>.

[10] Judge Paul Pressler, *A Hill on Which to Die: One Southern Baptist's Journey* (Nashville: Broadman & Holman Publishers, 1999), x-xi.

[11] David S. Dockery, *The Doctrine of the Bible* (Nashville: Convention Press, 1991).

[12] Jerry Vines, "Eschatology: Premillennial or Amillennial?" in *The Theological Educator* 37 (Spring 1988): 134.

[13] Patterson, "Stalemate," 2.

[14] The Southern Baptist Convention will address the committee's recommendation to withdraw from the Baptist World Alliance at its meeting in June 2004.

CHAPTER 6

RELATING TO FUNDAMENTALISTS

One of the challenges progressive Baptists face is to relate to Fundamentalists in a Christian manner. Assuming the likelihood that the two groups will not be reconciled in the present generation, what options are available and what guidelines do we have for choosing the best option?

These are not questions we can avoid, since we will be together with Fundamentalists in our churches, in local Baptist associations, in state Baptist conventions, in national Baptist bodies, and in the Baptist World Alliance. In addition, many of us encounter Fundamentalists in our families and extended families, in our neighborhoods, at our places of work, and in our social and civic clubs. Even if we avoid Fundamentalists in these settings, we will encounter them in the wider world. Their spokespeople will be interviewed on CNN, and elsewhere in public life they will be contending for the hearts and minds of our fellow citizens. Fundamentalists are not going away, and we need to develop a philosophy about how we can best relate to them. Although we cannot control how Fundamentalists relate to us, we are responsible to decide how we will relate to them.

A Secure Place

An important first step toward relationships with Fundamentalists is to be secure in our faith. For most Christians, this means we must be informed and thoughtful about our faith, and it means we must attempt to practice our faith with integrity.

Various kinds of experiences can erode security in our faith. One example is the occurrence of profound suffering in our lives or in the lives of those we love; another is an unexpected, dramatic failure in our lives. There are others.

We are concerned about the way in which our encounters with Fundamentalism can erode our confidence in the way we live out our Christian faith. We believe many non-Fundamentalist Christians have looked at Fundamentalists and said, "Those people really believe, and they really practice what they believe. I know I don't believe and practice what they do, and I don't want to. I wonder if this means I'm not a real Christian, or at least not a good one." Most of us do not express this verbally; it is something we feel more than think.

It isn't difficult to understand why we have feelings like this. After all, Fundamentalists do believe things deeply, and they do practice them energetically.

However, even though these feelings are understandable, they are mistaken. It simply isn't the case that Fundamentalists are the only Christians or the only good Christians. Fundamentalism is one expression of the Christian faith; it is *not* the only one. After all, the Christian faith existed and was practiced for nineteen centuries before the rise of Fundamentalism. These earlier forms of Christian faith have not been rendered obsolete or inferior by the rise of Fundamentalism.

In fact, we believe many of these other expressions of the Christian faith are superior to Fundamentalism. Because Fundamentalism often does not successfully identify what the fundamentals of the Christian faith are, and because it has often endorsed attitudes that are destructive of Christian community, we think there are better expressions of Christian faith than Fundamentalism. We think progressive Baptist beliefs and practices are among these better expressions.

We want to be clear here. We are not saying that individual Fundamentalists are inferior Christians. On the contrary, we know that there are many devoted, sincere Fundamentalist Christians, and we are grateful that this is the case. But we think that, though there are many fine individual Fundamentalists, the Fundamentalist impulse and movement have tended to miss the fundamentals of the Christian faith and to work against the unity and harmony of the church.

We think progressive Baptists have a stronger grasp of the fundamentals of the Christian faith and contribute more to the unity and harmony of the church than Fundamentalists. One of the reasons we have dedicated this book to President Jimmy Carter is that he repeatedly and consistently has related to Fundamentalists in a truly Christian manner.

Fellow Christians

We believe it is important for progressive Baptists to recognize that Fundamentalists are fellow Christians who are sincerely attempting to do what they believe is right. One of the ways to dehumanize other Christians is to suggest that they are not real Christians or not sincere Christians. This is a step Fundamentalists have sometimes taken toward progressive Baptists, and it is one that progressive Baptists should not take toward Fundamentalists.

Underlying this conviction is an understanding of what it means to be a Christian, and we are happy to identify our understanding of this basic idea. We understand a Christian to be a person who has heard the gospel that Christ died for our sins and rose again[1] and who has responded to that message by placing his or her trust in Jesus Christ as savior and lord. Progressive Baptists have done this; Fundamentalists have done it also, so progressive Baptists should recognize them as fellow Christians.

Kindness

How should progressive Baptists treat Fundamentalists? The answer is simple: they should treat them in a Christian way. A part of what it means to treat people in a Christian way is to be kind. Kindness is not a characteristic for which Fundamentalists are usually known. We think kindness should be characteristic of progressive Baptists.

One needed expression of kindness is to refuse to attribute to Fundamentalism the problems found among the fundamentalisms in other religions. For example, while we do not agree with the new directions taken by the Southern Baptist Convention, we certainly distinguish between them and the violence of, for example, some Islamic fundamentalists. We believe that a failure to make such distinctions is morally flawed in a profound way.

Forgiveness

During the controversy in Southern Baptist life, many progressive Baptists were deeply hurt. Untrue and unkind things were said about them, their reputations were diminished, their lives were disrupted, and some of them were deprived of their places of ministry and their incomes.[2]

Fortunately, time is mending some of their pain, but there are limits to what time alone can do. Christians have a special resource when they have been mistreated; Christ taught his followers to forgive their enemies.[3]

Forgiveness means experiencing pain of two kinds. First, you experience the pain of being hurt by others. Second, you experience the pain that comes from refusing to follow your natural instinct, which is to hit back at those who have hurt you.

Forgiveness has the power to end the destructive cycle set in motion by those who hurt you. It does this by healing your pain so that you no longer want to hit back at your enemies. Forgiveness is difficult work because it doesn't come naturally to any of us; what comes naturally is retaliation. But forgiveness is possible, and once it has been achieved, it mends our hearts.[4]

To forgive those who have hurt us does not mean to allow them to go on hurting us. Jesus called us to forgive our enemies; he did not call us to remain in harm's way.[5] We think the principal Christian response when we are hurt is to get out of harm's way. We recognize that on some occasions we will choose to make sacrifices for others, but it is we who are to make that choice, not our enemies. In all of this, Jesus is our pattern; he was willing to give his life for others, but only on his own terms: "No one takes [my life] from me, but I lay it down of my own accord."[6]

Forgiveness is not the same thing as reconciliation. Forgiveness is something you can do alone, without any assistance from the person who has hurt you. Supported by God and the church, you can, in the privacy of your own heart, forgive those who have hurt you.

Reconciliation, however, is not something you can achieve on your own. It takes two to be reconciled. Reconciliation is possible only when you forgive those who hurt you and when they acknowledge that they have hurt you and are willing to accept your forgiveness. Sometimes it is impossible to be reconciled to those who hurt us; certainly that is the case when those who hurt us have died. But even then, we can forgive them in our hearts, even though we can never in this life be reconciled with them.

Forgiveness is an indispensable component in the way progressive Baptists who were hurt during the controversy must relate to Fundamentalists.

Time for Healing

Although separatism is characteristic of much Fundamentalism, it is not the Christian ideal. Jesus' desire for his disciples is "that they may all be one."[7]

But sometimes this ideal is not possible, and we suspect that is the case for many progressive Baptists today. Disengaging from Fundamentalists may be the best option available for them at the present time. Disengagement should not come because they do not believe that Fundamentalists are Christians or because they refuse to accept offers of cooperation from Fundamentalists. Rather, given the pain and grief experienced by many progressive Baptists over the last quarter-century, it may be best for them to disengage from Fundamentalists long enough for their wounds to heal.

In the meantime, progressive Baptists can find and work with other fellow Christians who want to work with them. There are many Baptists around the world who have not accepted the beliefs or attitudes of Fundamentalism. In addition, progressive Baptists have a lot in common with non-Fundamentalists of other denominations. In many places, progressive Baptists are engaging in a new kind of ecumenism; they are building bridges to Christians who have rejected the theology and attitudes of Fundamentalism. We believe that kind of ecumenism holds great promise.

Resistance

Martin Luther King Jr. taught the American church and nation the power of nonviolent resistance. As a Christian minister, he appealed to Jesus Christ as the prime example of nonviolent resistance. He wrote, "It was Jesus of Nazareth that stirred the Negroes to protest with the creative weapon of love."[8] We think nonviolent resistance is an appropriate response to Fundamentalism.

In an early article on nonviolence, Dr. King made five points about nonviolent resistance. First, it is not cowardly; it does resist. Second, it does not seek to defeat or humiliate opponents, but to win their friendship and understanding. Third, it is directed against forces of evil rather than against people who are caught in those forces. Fourth, it avoids not only external physical violence but also the internal violence of spirit. Finally, it is based on the conviction that the universe is on the side of justice.[9]

This understanding of nonviolent resistance underlies our convictions about how progressive Baptists should resist the destructive tendencies in some expressions of Fundamentalism.

Where would this resistance be needed? What forms would it take? These are the two questions that we want to answer. First, this resistance is needed in personal relationships, church relationships, and societal relationships. In situations where Fundamentalists aggressively state their views and militantly seek to enforce them, it is appropriate for other Christians to resist them. There are times when refusal to resist Fundamentalism seems to us to be, as Dr. King said, "cowardly."

This resistance will take one of two primary forms. The most common form is argument. We believe there are venues in which we should engage Fundamentalists in debate. We should not allow them to misstate the truth, and we should challenge them when they claim that their version of Christianity is the only genuine expression of the faith. It is our hope that this book will provide help for those who are in a situation in which they are called upon to debate with Fundamentalists.

The other primary form of resistance is organization. That was the secret of the success of the civil rights movement; its proponents organized. We believe it is appropriate for progressive Baptists to organize in their churches, denominations, communities, and nation to the resist the destructive tendencies in Fundamentalism. The organization of the Cooperative Baptist Fellowship by former Southern Baptists is, we think, a good example of how that may be done effectively.

Conversation

When possible, and under appropriate circumstances, progressive Baptists may engage in conversations about the Bible and theology with Fundamentalists. Many former Fundamentalists have expressed appreciation for non-Fundamentalist friends who were willing to listen to them and talk to them about the Christian faith.

A corollary of this kind of engagement is humility about our beliefs and willingness to change them if we see a better way. The Christian message is absolute, but our understanding of it is not, and authentic conversation with others means we listen with an openness to hear a better understanding of God's truth than we presently possess. This does not mean we lack conviction, but rather we recognize that our humanity imposes limitations on us and our sinfulness distorts our understanding of God's truth. We cannot engage in authentic conversation with Fundamentalists unless we are prepared to entertain the possibility that there is some issue about which they are right and we are wrong. To entertain this possibility requires, as we said earlier, that we be secure in our faith.

It is difficult to generalize about the appropriate circumstances for engaging in conversation with Fundamentalists, and we suspect that there may be no set rules for recognizing those circumstances. All that we are trying to say is that there may be times when it is appropriate, and progressive Baptists need to be open to that.

Transcending the Controversy Theologically

Until recently, Southern Baptists were different from northern evangelical Christians in an important way. Southern Baptists were Protestant traditionalists whose theology had not been affected much by the battles between the Fundamentalists and the liberals; northern evangelicals were Protestant traditionalists whose theology had been maximally affected by those battles.

This, it seems to us, is no longer the case; the theology of progressive Baptists today has been deeply affected by the controversy that began in the Southern Baptist Convention in 1979, probably as deeply affected as the theology of northern evangelicals was by the controversies that began in the 1920s.

If we are right about this, then there is an important implication for progressive Baptists: they need to take steps to limit the effects of the controversy upon their theology. In particular, progressive Baptists should resist the temptation to think that the only substantive evaluation of a theological idea is whether it is Fundamentalist or progressive. While we recognize that this evaluation is sometimes appropriate, we think it is a blunt instrument for theological reflection and that we must incorporate other kinds of evaluation into our thinking.[10]

Here are examples of alternative evaluative scales for a theological claim: Is the claim biblical or unbiblical? Is it catholic or sectarian? Is it traditional or innovative? Is it thoughtful or thoughtless? Is it relevant today or irrelevant? Is it scholastic or vital? Is it consistent or self-contradictory? Is it attuned to our experience or tone-deaf to it? Does it lead to moral conduct or to immoral conduct? Does it balance the claims of this life and the future life or not? Does it balance the concerns of the individual and the community or not? These are only examples; the list could be extended.

The point is that part of what progressive Baptists need to do as they think about relating to Fundamentalism is to take steps to insure that their own theology is not deformed by their experiences of the controversy with Fundamentalism. A particularly pernicious temptation is to disown ideas just because Fundamentalists embrace them or to embrace ideas just because Fundamentalists disown them.

It would be unfortunate as well as ironic if progressive Baptists, in reacting against Fundamentalist mistakes, were so formed by Fundamentalism that they found themselves reduced to employing categories that have been provided by Fundamentalism or simply reacting against Fundamentalist theology.

NOTES

[1] 1 Corinthians 15:1-7.

[2] Some Fundamentalists also had painful experiences, of course, but, as we said earlier, we are writing this book for Christians who are not Fundamentalists.

[3] Matthew 6:7-15; 18:21-35.

[4] John Claypool, *Mending the Heart* (Cambridge: Cowley Publications, 1999), ch. 1.

[5] We understand his instructions in Matthew 5:38-41 to apply to situations in which it is impossible to get out of harm's way; in Jesus' lifetime that would have been the situation for many Jews since they were living under the Roman occupation.

[6] John 10:18.

[7] John 17:21.

[8] Martin Luther King Jr., *Stride toward Freedom* (New York: Harper & Row, 1958), 13.

[9] Martin Luther King Jr., "Nonviolence and Racial Justice," *The Christian Century* 74 (6 February 1957): 165-67.

[10] Several theologians have done extensive academic work to help American Christians transcend the simplistic evaluation of "liberal or conservative." See, for example, Jack Rogers, *Claiming the Center* (Louisville: Westminster John Knox Press, 1995); Douglas Jacobsen and William Vance Trollinger, Jr., "Evangelical and Ecumenical: Re-Forming a Center," *The Christian Century* (13-20 July 1994).

A BETTER WAY

We believe the way of progressive Baptists is a better way of following Christ today than the way of Fundamentalism, and in this conclusion we hope to show why this is the case.

The Four Enemies

We have seen that Fundamentalism is a loose coalition formed to conduct a war against the Enlightenment, biblical criticism, evolution, and liberal theology, which were understood as the thin edge of the wedge of secularism and unbelief.

In our judgment, resistance to secularism is important for all Christians. Christianity is a religion; religion and secularism are not compatible. We do not agree with all the ways Fundamentalists resisted secularism, but we do agree with them that Christianity is opposed to secularism.

We think Fundamentalists made a mistake when they assumed that the four enemies were intractably secular. We think there are true and valuable ideas in each one, and that in evaluating each one it is important to distinguish between what is true and what is not true.

The Enlightenment made many important contributions to modern life, some good and some not good. Its affirmation of the rights of individuals should be welcomed, though not its excessive emphasis on individualism to the exclusion of community. Its call for the liberation of individuals from the tyranny of authorities was good; the divine right of kings to rule was a form of political tyranny, and we all should welcome modern liberal democracy with its embrace of human rights. Sometimes the authority of the church did operate in a tyrannical way, and it is a good thing that individual Christians today are encouraged to think about things for themselves. The Enlightenment's affirmation that people should employ their reason to understand their world and to overcome superstitions was right, though the Enlightenment thinkers who reduced all human understanding to what can be grasped by reason alone were wrong. The Enlightenment was right in affirming the possibilities of progress, though a more Christian understanding of progress is that God is working in the world to lead it to its true destiny.

We today should appreciate the good things the Enlightenment set in motion, even as we express our reservations about its limitations and errors.

The same is true of biblical criticism. Fundamentalists were mistaken to reject it totally; what they should have done was to discern its good contributions from its errors and embrace the former and not the latter. In *The Fundamentals*, Dyson Hague did this, but in later Fundamentalism biblical criticism was rejected in its entirety. The truth is that all of the Christian church has benefited from this modern way of studying the Bible, even the Fundamentalists, and it is ungrateful not to acknowledge this.

Of course, biblical critics make mistakes; this is only to be expected, since all Christians make mistakes in interpreting the Bible. The possibility that mistakes may be made in biblical interpretation cannot justify a moratorium on biblical interpretation; what it does is provide an incentive for Christians to work harder to interpret the Bible more faithfully and carefully.

Moreover, biblical criticism is not the only way to study the Bible, and the biblical critics who have suggested that it is are mistaken. There are many ways to use the Bible so as to allow its message to grasp us. We may read it devotionally. We may memorize it. We may meditate upon it, repeating its words silently or aloud many times as a way of internalizing them, digesting them for spiritual food. We may see parts of the Bible enacted on stage or in movies, and we may hear the Bible sung as music. We may, as some ancient Jews did, carry written copies of portions of the Bible on our person as reminders of the message of God's word. Perhaps most important of all, we may hear the Bible read aloud in worship services and then proclaimed by preachers.

But when we recognize that biblical criticism has made mistakes and that it is not the only way to study the Bible, we ought not to forget how much we owe to it, and that should lead us to affirm its place in the life of the church.

The same thing may be said about evolution. In the minds of many people, including some atheists as well as Fundamentalists, modern evolutionary theory is intrinsically atheistic. Naturally, all Christians will resist atheism.

But we do not agree with the atheists and the Fundamentalists who say evolution is intrinsically atheistic. We think, in fact, that evolution can be incorporated faithfully into the Christian understanding of God as Creator of the world. This has been done by many Christians, among whom we mention John Polkinghorne as having been especially helpful to us.[1]

Finally, we do not agree with the comprehensive rejection of liberal theology by Fundamentalists. Certainly liberal theologians have made mistakes, and those familiar with the course of Christian theology in the twentieth century have been alerted to problems of liberal theology. Harry Emerson Fosdick expressed this clearly:

> The conflict between liberal and reactionary Christianity had long been moving toward a climax. There were faults on both sides. The modernists were tempted to make a supine surrender to prevalent cultural ideas, accepting them wholesale, and using them as the authoritative standard by which to judge the truth or falsity of classical Christian affirmations. The reactionaries, sensing the peril in this shift of authority, were tempted to retreat into hidebound obscurantism, denying the discoveries of science, and insisting on the literal acceptance of every Biblical idea, which even Christians of the ancient church had avoided by means of allegorical interpretations.[2]

This is especially impressive because Fosdick was the leading liberal minister of his era, and his 1922 sermon "Shall the Fundamentalists Win?" is probably the single most famous document opposing Fundamentalism in the 1920s.[3] The point is that there were good and bad things in liberal theology, and what was needed was not a comprehensive rejection of it, such as Fundamentalists offered, but a discriminating evaluation of what was true in it and what was not.

In summary, Fundamentalism was right in its rejection of secularism, but its understanding and evaluation of the Enlightenment, biblical criticism, evolution, and liberal theology were defective.

The Fundamentals

Although we believe Fundamentalists are sincere in their beliefs, we also believe they have misunderstood what is truly fundamental in the Christian faith. In our judgment, the beliefs they offer as fundamental are, in fact, supplementary beliefs, not the fundamentals of the Christian faith.

Fundamentalists are like an army that sets up outposts to defend a city and then begins to think the outposts are themselves the city. It isn't the inerrancy of the Scriptures that is most fundamental; it is the authority of the Bible for the faith and life of Christians. It isn't the virgin birth of Christ that is most fundamental; it is the Incarnation. It isn't the penal substitutionary atonement theory that is most fundamental; it is the glorious gospel that Christ died to save the world. It isn't the historicity of the miracles in the Bible that is most fundamental; it is God's power to govern the world. It isn't the premillennial view of the second coming that is most fundamental; it is that God's will is going to be done "on Earth as it is in heaven."[4] It is not the denial of evolution that is most fundamental; it is the affirmation that God is the Creator of the universe.

The same sort of thing may be said about more recent Fundamentalist affirmations. For example, it is not the submission of wives to their husbands that is most fundamental; it is the affirmation that God wants husbands and wives to love each other.

If these are not the fundamentals of the Christian faith, what are the fundamentals? Every Christian has the responsibility to try to answer that question for himself or herself, and those of us who are in churches that affirm our freedom to think for ourselves are fortunate.

It is our judgment that, as we think about what is most fundamental in our faith, we need to be in conversation with the entire Christian church and not only with the Fundamentalist segment of it. It seems to us that it is possible to describe what the entire, undivided church has affirmed as the fundamentals of our faith. While people express these differently, we offer the following as one account of what the entire church has affirmed:

Monotheism: There is one and only one true and living God.

Creation: God created the universe out of nothing.

The Fall: Human beings have fallen into sin.

The Trinity: In some wonderful and mysterious way, the one true God is Father, Son, and Holy Spirit.

Incarnation: God loved the world and sent his Son into the world.

The Gospel: Jesus taught people, healed them, and died and rose again to save them.

Pentecost: God poured out the Holy Spirit on the followers of Jesus.

Mission: The Spirit guides and empowers the entire church on its work in the world.

Word and Sacrament: The church preaches the gospel, baptizes, and observes the Lord's Supper.

Christian Hope: God will complete all this work in the future.

Scripture: The Bible tells us the wonderful story of God.

These beliefs are shared by Eastern Orthodox Christians, by Roman Catholics, and by Protestants of all kinds, so they have an ecumenical rather than a sectarian character. All of them are deeply embedded in the Scriptures, and, in fact, we believe they are a rounded and balanced account of the biblical revelation. The Archbishop of Canterbury, Rowan Williams, has described beliefs such as these as tradition *in its power and fullest sense* and not as a *lifeboat in which to escape the present.*[5]

We think these beliefs are more fundamental than those offered by Fundamentalism, and we believe the entire church is a better guide to the fundamentals of our Christian faith than the Fundamentalists. We think Fundamentalism is too shallow. What the church needs today is a deeper, richer understanding of what the Christian faith is about than that offered by Fundamentalism.

In that sense, we are catholic Christians, or ecumenical Christians, believing that we can best grasp the fundamentals of Christianity by entering into conversation with the entire church.

We also are Baptist Christians, and we treasure the Baptist legacy of freedom.[6] For this reason, we think that the only appropriate ways to disseminate and defend our catholic and ecumenical understanding of the Christian fundamentals are ways that respect the freedom of listeners to think about the fundamentals for themselves. In our judgment, Fundamentalism lacks a good grasp on Christian freedom. Paul's counsel to the Galatians is relevant here: "For freedom Christ has set us free. Stand firm, therefore, and do not submit again to a yoke of slavery."[7] Paul was talking about freedom from legalism in his era; we assume that his words are appropriately applied to freedom from legalisms in any era, including our own.

In summary, we believe in catholic substance united with Baptist freedom.

Conclusion

By now our readers are aware that we think of Fundamentalists as fellow Christians who are attempting sincerely to do what they believe is right and that, moreover, they are right about some things, such as that traditional Christian faith is incompatible with a secular understanding of reality.

Nevertheless, we do not think Fundamentalism is the best expression of the Christian faith, either in terms of its theology or its characteristic attitudes, and we want to close our book by inviting readers to consider an alternative expression, one that is not "imprisoned in anti-modernism," to borrow a memorable phrase from a book by Hans Küng.[8]

We believe trust in God is the most wonderful thing that can happen to a person, and Jesus has made it possible for us to trust in God. He has done this by his own trust in his Father, by his teachings, and by his sacrificial death and resurrection from the dead. Jesus' Spirit has made this good news a living reality in our experience, and our trust in God is nurtured and challenged in the fellowship of the Christian church. The church includes all of the children of God, and the harmony of its common life depends upon its members' forbearance toward each other as they live their lives in the magnificent freedom Christ has given them. The essence of the church's life is to love God and to love other people, as Jesus taught us. The church possesses a confident hope that the future belongs to God just as the past and the present do. This hope supports the church as it attempts to live out its love for other people through missions, evangelism, and education, and through ministries of compassion, justice, and peacemaking.

We are committed to Jesus, his Father, and their Spirit, and we are confident that today as in the past, the best guidelines for living out this commitment are faith, hope, and love.

NOTES

[1] John Polkinghorne has written nearly thirty books, most of them accessible to non-scientists. For a sense of his theology and its relationship to science in general, see his *Belief in God in an Age of Science* (New Haven: Yale University Press, 1998).

[2] Harry Emerson Fosdick, *The Living of These Days* (New York: Harper & Row, Publishers, 1956), 144.

[3] Harry Emerson Fosdick, "Shall the Fundamentalists Win?: Defending Liberal Protestantism in the 1920s," *Christian Work* 102 (June 10, 1922): 716-722.

[4] Matthew 6:10.

[5] These phrases are being used by a movement within Anglicanism and may be found at that movement's website: <http://www.affirmingcatholicism.org/us/default.html>.

[6] Walter B. Shurden, *The Baptist Identity: Four Fragile Freedoms* (Macon: Smyth & Helwys Publishing, Inc., 1993).

[7] Galatians 5:1.

[8] Hans Küng, *My Struggle for Freedom: Memoirs*, trans. John Bowden (Grand Rapids: William B. Eerdmans Publishing Company, 2002), 262.

GUIDE FOR INDIVIDUAL STUDY OR GROUP DISCUSSION

Introduction: Getting Our Bearings

The authors wrote this book for people who want to understand Fundamentalism, and they hope it will help readers to be strong in their faith and to be able to relate to Fundamentalists in a Christian way.

(1) What questions do you have about Fundamentalism?

(2) Do people who leave Fundamentalism also leave the Christian faith entirely?

(3) What is the difference between Fundamentalism and fundamentalism?

Chapter 1: Generic Fundamentalism

In this chapter the authors identify family resemblances shared by Fundamentalist movements in many religions.

(1) Could there be an atheistic form of fundamentalism? Why or why not?

(2) Was there fundamentalism in the ancient world? Why or why not?

(3) Why do you think virtually all fundamentalist leaders are males?

(4) Do you think cooperation between fundamentalists and others is ever possible?

(5) Have you observed some of these characteristics in fundamentalists you have known?

(6) Are all fundamentalists militant? Are they all violent? What is the difference?

Chapter 2: The Original Fundamentalism

In this chapter the authors give a description and a brief sketch of the history of Protestant Fundamentalism in the United States.

(1) What is the most surprising fact you learned in this chapter?

(2) What is your stance toward the four ideas associated with the Enlightenment?

(3) Do you think it is appropriate to study the Bible critically? Why or why not?

(4) Do you think it is reasonable for people who believe God created human beings in God's own image to accept the idea that human beings evolved from lower forms of life? Why or why not?

(5) Do you think liberal theology always leads to secularism and unbelief? Why or why not?

(6) How do you think Fundamentalists felt when, following their defeats in the 1920s, they lost their dominant role in American society and came to be treated with contempt by many Americans?

(7) What do you think are the principal differences between Fundamentalists and evangelicals?

(8) How would you explain the reemergence of Fundamentalism in the late 1970s?

(9) Do you agree that we are all minorities now? *If not, why not? If so, what are the implications of this idea?*

Chapter 3: The Theology of Fundamentalism

In this chapter the authors describe some of the doctrinal beliefs of Fundamentalists. They believe the Fundamentalists' claim to be deeply concerned about theology, but they point out that it is difficult to pin down Fundamentalist theology precisely.

(1) The authors say there is a big difference between theological writings, which are written to help readers understand ideas, and polemical writings, which are written to defend ideas. Do you agree?

(2) Do you find Dyson Hague's view of biblical criticism convincing? Why or why not?

(3) Were you surprised by James Orr's view of evolution? What do you think of his view?

(4) Do you agree with the writers that the Five Fundamentals are not fundamental enough? If so, what do you think is more fundamental than these five themes?

(5) Do you think 2 Timothy 3:16 is a sufficient statement about the Bible? If not, what would you want to add to it?

(6) Do you agree with the authors that the Bible contains many understandings of the meaning of Jesus' sufferings, death, and resurrection?

(7) Fundamentalists have a particular understanding of the end of the world, namely, premillennialism. Do you think it is important to have a particular understanding of what will happen at the end of the world? If so, what is your understanding? If not, what do you think Christians need to believe about the future?

(8) If someone asked you to list the Christian fundamentals as you understand them, what would be on your list?

Chapter 4: The Attitudes of Fundamentalism

In this chapter the authors review attitudes that are frequently, if not universally, found among Fundamentalists. They also describe the problems with these attitudes and alternatives to these attitudes.

(1) Do you agree that, in order to understand Fundamentalism, you must understand its attitudes as well as its history and theology?

(2) When you see Fundamentalists on television or are among Fundamentalists you know personally, have you observed tendencies toward the following: suspicion? fear? anger? separatism?

(3) Should Christians ever be suspicious of other people? Why or why not?

(4) Were you ever warned against being changed by higher education? How did you respond?

(5) Do you think the church today has things it should fear? If so, what? If not, why not?

(6) Is there a difference between anger and righteous indignation? Do you think anger is an ideal motivation for Christians? Why or why not?

(7) Is separatism ever appropriate for Christians? If you think it sometimes is, how do you know when it is appropriate and when it is not?

(8) Do you agree with President Carter that breaking through the barrier and reaching out to others is what personifies a Christian? *Why or why not?*

Chapter 5: Fundamentalism and Southern Baptists

In this chapter the authors review the recent controversy in the Southern Baptist Convention as a case study of Fundamentalism. They ask whether, if we set rhetoric aside, it is accurate to use the word *Fundamentalist* to describe the new directions in the Convention.

(1) Were you surprised to learn that Southern Baptists resisted Fundamentalism for most of the twentieth century?

(2) Have you ever heard a combative preacher who seemed to you to be like J. Frank Norris? If so, did that preacher's message help you?

(3) Do you have a personal tie to the Southern Baptist Convention? If so, how did this chapter make you feel? If not, did the story in this chapter remind you of anything in your church or denomination?

(4) Do you agree that the new directions in the Southern Baptist Convention since 1979 may be fairly described as Fundamentalist? Why or why not? If you agree, do you think it is a good idea to say publicly that the new directions are Fundamentalist? Why or why not?

(5) What are your feelings about the Southern Baptist Convention firing missionaries who did not accept the new policy concerning women in ministry?

Chapter 6: Relating to Fundamentalists

In this chapter the authors make suggestions about how progressive Baptists can relate to Fundamentalists.

(1) The authors say they think some Christians have been made to feel insecure by the way in which Fundamentalists live out their faith. Have you observed this?

(2) Do you think of Fundamentalists as fellow Christians?

(3) Fundamentalism is frequently militant. Do you think it is realistic of the authors to propose that progressive Baptists should be kind toward Fundamentalists? Do you think it is difficult to be kind to Fundamentalists? Why or why not?

111

(4) Do you agree that people who were hurt during the controversy may find it difficult to forgive those who hurt them? Why or why not?

(5) Do you think the authors are right to suggest that those who were hurt in the controversy may need time for healing to take place?

(6) What happens when you talk to Fundamentalists? Do you have ideas about how best to engage them?

(7) Do you agree with Martin Luther King, Jr. that it is possible to resist without resorting to violence?

(8) Have you ever wondered whether you are too preoccupied with the categories of liberal/conservative? Do you find other categories helpful? If so, which ones?

Conclusion: A Better Way

(1) The authors say that Christians should firmly resist secularism but that they should appreciate what is good in the Enlightenment, biblical criticism, evolution, and liberal theology. Do you agree? Why or why not?

(2) How can Christians share their faith without becoming argumentative or condescending?

(3) Do you agree with Harry Emerson Fosdick that there were faults on both sides *of the Fundamentalist/Modernist controversy? Do you think that is true today also?*

(4) The authors provided a list of what they consider to be Christian fundamentals; do you find this list helpful? If you were drawing up a list, what would you put on it?

(5) What did you find most helpful in this book, if anything? With what in this book did you most disagree?